LOOP HIKES
Colorado

BEST LOOP HIKES
Colorado

Steve Johnson & David Weinstein

THE MOUNTAINEERS BOOKS

THE MOUNTAINEERS BOOKS
is the nonprofit publishing arm of The Mountaineers Club, an organization founded in 1906 and dedicated to the exploration, preservation, and enjoyment of outdoor and wilderness areas.

1001 SW Klickitat Way, Suite 201, Seattle, WA 98134

First edition, 2006

Manufactured in the United States of America

Acquiring Editor: Cassandra Conyers
Project Editor: Laura Drury
Copy Editor: Brenda Pittsley
Cover and Book Design: The Mountaineers Books
Layout: Mayumi Thompson
Cartographer: Moore Creative Designs
Photographer: All photographs by the authors unless otherwise noted.

Cover photograph: *Gunnison National Forest* © William Manning/Corbis
Frontispiece: *Indian Paintbrush*

Maps shown in this book were produced using National Geographic's *TOPO!* software. For more information, go to *www.nationalgeographic. com/topo*.

Library of Congress Cataloging-in-Publication Data
Johnson, Steve, 1965-
  Best loop hikes Colorado / by Steve Johnson and David Weinstein.-- 1st ed.
    p. cm.
  ISBN 0-89886-978-1 (pbk.)
  1. Hiking--Colorado--Guidebooks. 2. Colorado--Guidebooks. I. Weinstein, David.
II. Title.
  GV199.42.C6J64 2005
  796.51'09788--dc22
                                      2005025588

For Jack & Lauren
and
Lee & Nancy

CONTENTS

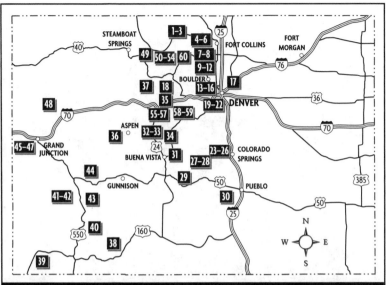

══════ Interstate highway	🛡90 Interstate
────── Paved road	〔97〕 U.S. highway
══════ Unpaved road	⬭410 State or County road
·············· Featured trail	▭9712 Forest road
‑ ‑ ‑ ‑ ‑ Connecting trail	🅣 Trailhead
·············· Cross-country trail	P Parking
River/creek	▲ Campground or Site
Lake	) (Pass/saddle
∽ Spring	▲ Peak
⊼ Picnic area	■ Building
][Bridge	

Map locations referenced: 1-3, 4-6, 7-8, 9-12, 13-16, 17, 18, 19-22, 23-26, 27-28, 29, 30, 31, 32-33, 34, 35, 36, 37, 38, 39, 40, 41-42, 43, 44, 45-47, 48, 49, 50-54, 55-57, 58-59, 60

Cities: STEAMBOAT SPRINGS, FORT COLLINS, FORT MORGAN, BOULDER, DENVER, ASPEN, GRAND JUNCTION, BUENA VISTA, COLORADO SPRINGS, GUNNISON, PUEBLO

Hike Summary Table

Hike Number and Name	Distance (miles)	Hiking Time (hours or days)	Elevation Gain (feet)	Season	Highlight
1 Mount McConnel Trail	4.3	2.5 – 3 hours	2256	April through November	Poudre Canyon, quiet wilderness
2 Greyrock Trail	6.5	3 – 4 hours	2694	Year-round	Mountain meadow, boulder playground on summit
3 Dowdy Lake	2.2	1 hour	51	April through October	Red Feather Lakes, chimney rock formations
4 Arthurs Rock	5.9	5 hours	2439	April through October	Horsetooth Reservoir, great views of plains
5 Horsetooth Mountain Trail	4.5	3 hours	1392	April through November	Forested hogbacks, fun climb to Horsethooth summit
6 ELC Loop	2.8	1 hour	10	April through October	Raptor Center, wetlands, prairie, lots of wildlife
7 Devils Backbone Trail	4	3 hours	400	April through October	Rugged Devils Backbone formation
8 Eagle Wind Trail	4	3.25 hours	418	April through October	Critical wildlife habitat, views of Longs Peak and Flatirons
9 Red Rock Loop	8	4.5 hours	1477	June through October	St. Vrain Creek, secluded woods
10 Bear Peak Loop	6.2	4.5 hours	2998	May through October	Hogback ridges, canyons, great eastern views
11 Mount Sanitas	3.4	2+ hours	1343	April through October	Great in-town hike
12 Boulder Valley Ranch	3.2	1.5 – 2 hours	320	Year-round	Trail run, mountain bike, natural wetland, views of Boulder
13 Burro Loop	5.4	2 – 3 hours	1920	May through October	Close to Boulder, nice views of plains and mountains
14 Walker Ranch	7.6	3 hours	1931	March through November	Open valleys, dense woods, just far enough from town
15 Canyon Loop	3.2	1.5 hours	380	Year-round	Rolling hills, sweeping vistas
16 Devils Thumb	14.7	12 hours	3394	May through September	Continental Divide, long-distance views, wildflowers

Hike Number and Name	Distance (miles)	Hiking Time (hours or days)	Elevation Gain (feet)	Season	Highlight
17 Barr Lake State Park	8.8	3.5 hours	113	Year-round	Bird-watchers paradise, easy hike close to Denver
18 White Ranch Park	4.8	2 – 3 hours	1677	April through November	Lots of wildlife, great eastern views, beautiful state park
19 Lodgepole Loop	2.3	1 hour	1508	March through October	Easy hike close to Denver, loaded with wildflowers
20 Fountain Valley Trail	2.8	1.5 hours	373	Year-round	Fantastic geology, wildlife galore
21 Evergreen Mountain Loop	4.3	2.5 hours	1056	March to December	Rolling hills, secluded trails, close to Evergreen Loop
22 South Valley Park	2.9	1.5 hours	1370	Year-round	Red stone rock formations, critical elk habitat
23 Garden of the Gods	1.5	1 hour	401	April through October	Humbling rock towers, multiple "hidden" loops, nice visitor center
24 Queens Canyon	3	2.5 – 3 hours	1499	May through October	Narrow canyon trail, waterfall, ridgeline views of Pikes Peak
25 The Incline	3	1.5 hours	2011	May through October	Daunting challenge on one-of-a-kind trail, cog railroad, Pikes Peak
26 Waldo Canyon	6.2	2 – 2.5 hours	2070	May through October	Excellent path through forested foothills, close to Colorado Springs
27 Lovell Gulch Trail	5	2.5 – 3 hours	951	June through October	Quiet trail, views of Pikes Peak, close to Woodland Park
28 Cheesman Ranch	12	6 hours	536	May through October	Meadows, forests, old ranch buildings, nice campsites
29 Beaver Creek Loop	6.9	4.5 hours	1486	Year-round	Diverse plant and animal life, high canyon walls
30 Pueblo Mountain Park	2.8	1.5 – 2 hours	1008	May through October	Open hills, dense woods, Environmental Center

HIKE SUMMARY TABLE (CONTINUED)

Hike Number and Name	Distance (miles)	Hiking Time (hours or days)	Elevation Gain (feet)	Season	Highlight
31 Petrified Forest Loop	1.5	45 minutes	80	Year-round	Fossils of animals and redwoods
32 Fancy Pass Trail	8.5	5 – 6 hours	2584	June through October	High alpine lakes, deep gorges, stunning views of surrounding mountains
33 Mount of the Holy Cross	15	11+ hours	6790	June through October	Epic trek over rugged ridgeline, giant fourteener, stunning views
34 Four Score	7	4 – 5 hours	3422	July through October	Four fourteeners in one day
35 Ptarmigan Trail	7	5 hours	2605	June through October	Great trail through aspen and pine, views of Dillon Reservoir
36 Crater Lake Trail	3.6	2 hours	698	June through October	Exquisite views of Maroon Bells, fun trail through aspen groves
37 Eaglesmere Loop	9.3	6 hours	1800	June through October	Lush forests, great views of gnarly, unnamed peaks
38 Fourmile Falls	11	6 hours	2850	June through October	Over a dozen waterfalls, secluded lake for mid-hike rest
39 Petroglyph Point Trail	2.8	2 hours	554	Year-round	Petroglyphs, Anasazi history, cliff dwellings
40 Storms Gulch Trail	5.75	3 hours	2306	June through October	Incredible views of Sneffels Range and vicinity, Ouray
41 Jud Wiebe Trail	3.3	2.5 hours	1517	May through October	Bridal Veil Falls, some of best alpine scenery in Colorado, Telluride
42 Wilson Mesa Loop	5.5	2.5 hours	1415	May through September	Wilson Peak, wildflowers, Telluride
43 Portland Trail	3.5	2.5 hours	1050	June through October	Rugged mountain scenery, huge mountain amphitheater, Ouray
44 Oak Flat Loop	1.2	45 minutes	400	May through October	Really cool canyon—check out Warner Point and the Painted Wall
45 Devils Canyon Loop	6.5	3.5 hours	670	Year-round	Desert land of canyon walls, massive columns of rock, and open, red valleys

Hike Number and Name	Distance (miles)	Hiking Time (hours or days)	Elevation Gain (feet)	Season	Highlight
46 Pollock Bench Trail	5.5	3 hours	967	Year-round	Magnificent canyons, vast mesas, and deep winding gorges
47 Mary Moore Loop	9.5	5 hours	1425	Year-round	Colorado River basin, Book Cliffs, Grand Mesa
48 Wall Lake Loop	14	10 hours	2180	June through September	The Flat Tops, three huge valleys, amazing wildflowers
49 Gilpin Lake Loop	10.5	6 hours	2417	May through October	Continental Divide, Mount Zirkel
50 Gem Lake Loop	10.8	5.5 hours	3523	May through October	Magical woodlands, soothing creeks, Gem Lake
51 Triple Threat	8	7 hours	4185	June through October	Three big summits, alpine tundra, beauteous views all around
52 Little Matterhorn	16	1 to 2 days	3226	June through October	Moraine Park, peaks of the Divide, pretty mountain streams, nice backcountry campsites
53 Bierstadt Lake Loop	3.5	2+ hours	756	June through October	Glacier Basin, grandeur of Bear Lake area
54 Onahu Creek Trail	7	4.5 hours	1817	May through October	Kawuneeche Valley, Never Summer mountains
55 Powderhound Trail	2.75	2.5 hours	529	December through March	Winter hike atop Continental Divide
56 Jackal Hut	9.1	6.5 hours	2415	December through March	Expansive Vail Pass Recreation Area, backcountry hut, unforgettable views
57 Highline Loop	7.1	4.5 hours	1350	December through April	Mount Massive, quiet woods near Leadville
58 Deadhorse Creek	7	3.5 hours	2710	December through April	Fraser Valley, two wilderness areas, solitude
59 10th Mountain Hut Trail	7.3	4+ hours	1205	December through April	10th Mountain Hut, Colorado Trail
60 Sprague Lake Loop	2.15	1.5 hours	262	Year-round	Easy snowshoe hike for beginners, great views of the Divide

PREFACE

As just a young buck, I was prone to making declarations of exploring every single place of majestic grandeur on the globe. I would read of a place, stare at tantalizing photos and say, "Yep, I'm going to be there someday." My lofty plans, however, always seemed to return to one venue—the mountains. It was there that grand adventure was sure to be found, with magnificently rugged peaks, enchanting streams, and high alpine forests. Even in only a picture, the land up high captivated and inspired.

A family trip as a young teen brought me to Colorado, and I walked right into my daydreams. The sky is transcendent blue, the delicate high-altitude air invigorates, and forests of pine smell like wintergreen candy. This is truly a magical place, and this book is a celebration of Colorado as seen from the soles of our hiking boots. There is a lifetime of trails to peruse here, but we chose sixty of some of the best loop hikes that delve into the state's most luxuriant locales. These trails offer a chance to get away for a short trek to stretch your legs a bit, or for a multiday journey to refresh your soul. The trails travel through Colorado's natural treasures like Rocky Mountain National Park and the Great Sand Dunes. They roam quietly with vagabond creeks, saunter through pageants of wildflowers, and soar with high mountain summits. We hope you enjoy our efforts, and most of all, that you take some time very soon to get out on the trails and wander.

Special thanks to my co-author and good buddy, David Weinstein. His fierce passion for the high country rivals my own, and our season of researching trails was simply unforgettable. There were frosty nights on the Rio Grande; tenacious, middle-of-the-night road trips in search of the next trail; tripping over a rock onto a moose carcass; and epic marches to the highest reaches of the state. Cheers, my friend.

—*Steve Johnson*, Spring 2005

The magnificent Maroon Bells

INTRODUCTION

Go outside and play—it's a familiar mantra of so many childhoods from when we were stir-crazy and making our parents crazier. Get out there and let off some steam. And so we did, exploring and creating and imagining, embarking on great adventures in the backyard or in a secret copse of woods. That wanderlust spirit still holds true for many of us when we grow up; we just want a bigger playground.

How about an entire state's worth of recess? Colorado is an outdoor lover's dream come true. It is all of our kid adventures come to life in extra large portions. The miniature field of neighborhood prairie is now the wind-rippled ocean of tall grasses and gentle waves of hills of the eastern plains. Our tiny homemade sandbox is now 30 square miles of the Great Sand Dunes National Park. Nearby hills we mightily conquered have grown to become the majestic Rocky Mountains, laden with hundreds of rugged peaks of soaring adventure. If your favorite place is outside, if you have adventure in your heart, your destination is here. Get out there and play!

Deep couloir in Rocky Mountain National Park

About Colorado

Colorado is a land of diversity. It's all here, from the vast eastern plains to the hogback ridges of the Front Range, from sprawling ranch land to the exquisite beauty of the high country, from rugged mountain summits to verdant valleys and peaceful streams. There is something for everyone, including unforgettable hiking trails.

Often overlooked as simply land between somewhere and the mountains, the eastern plains of Colorado make up some 40 percent of the state. Rising gradually from elevations as low as 3500 feet on the eastern border of the state, the golden plains make their way west to an abrupt greeting with the mountains. Mainly utilized for agriculture, the landscape relies heavily on the South Platte and Arkansas Rivers to feed this vast area of checkered bucolic beauty. But amidst the corn and wheat fields, Colorado has dedicated parts of these sprawling lands to conservation efforts like the Open Space Alliance to keep fragile ecosystems, wildlife habitat, and native areas undisturbed. (Some of these areas are open to hikers; others are simply set aside and spared from development.) On the plains, hikers can appreciate the vastness of Colorado by looking east to an undying sky, and west toward the highest reaches of the Rocky Mountains.

The beauty and diversity of Colorado's mountains hold their own with any mountain range in the world. With over one thousand peaks rising above 10,000 feet, and fifty-four above 14,000 feet, Colorado owns the highest average elevation in the United States. Five major mountain ranges run north to south. The Front Range and the Sangre de Cristos greet the Great Plains in a nearly continuous wall. Parallel to these eastern mountains, the Park, Sawatch, and San Juan Ranges run down the central part of the state. These two belts are made up of numerous smaller ranges and provide some of the best hiking and mountaineering on the globe. The Continental Divide runs down the eastern belt before moving to the west midstate. From this high point on the western side of the country, major rivers are formed and take very different paths. To the east, the Rio Grande, North and South Platte, and Arkansas Rivers begin their journeys toward the Atlantic Ocean. On the west side, in the high reaches of Rocky Mountain National Park, are the headwaters of the Colorado River, sending its virgin waters on a 1400-mile journey to the Pacific Ocean.

Similar to the plains in the east, the western plateau rises gently toward the Rocky Mountains. This ancient stretch of land is made of a chaotic array of mesas, plateaus, and smaller mountains. These are separated by the deep, cutting waters of rivers such as the Colorado and its chief tributaries, one of the biggest being the Gunnison River. The ongoing process of erosion continues to cut, shape, and form the beauty found out west. Painted canyons, deep gorges, stretching basins, and a plethora of alcoves are out there, ready to be explored and enjoyed. This part of the state hosts magnificent parks such as Dinosaur National Monument, Black Canyon of the Gunnison National Park, Colorado National Monument, and Mesa Verde National

Gem Lake in Rocky Mountain National Park

Park. Situated from north to south along the plateau, these parks allow easy access to loads of outdoor fun all along the western slope.

Our favorite way to explore is on foot, up close in these beautiful places, on a hiking trail wandering through the wilds. Or better yet, on a loopy path that is shiny and new with every step. A loop hike is a special treat. Every trail has its own unique characteristics, personalities if you will. There is something inherently mysterious about hiking a trail for the first time. It's like meeting a new friend, discovering his ups and downs and learning of hidden secrets. But best of all, it's about being together and having a good ol' time. A new trail makes a great friend, and we made a lot of them during the grueling research for this book. The anticipation of the unknown, the exploration of a new place, the hidden treasures around each bend, over every knoll—these discoveries keep us coming back again and again, to be with our new friends and share those discoveries. On a loop trail, newfound territory never ends, and it's like hiking the path for the first time, all the time.

Hiking is an activity that goes beyond the traditional goal of physical exercise. It allows us close contact with our favorite places, a chance for us to reach out and for the land to reach in with a comforting hand. The beauty of Colorado beckons for a time of reflection, or to challenge our spirit. A trek to a quiet, high mountain lake is the perfect undertaking. A mountain's stalwart indifference will test your mettle, and reward you mightily. A pair of boots and a pack can do wonders for easing life's ills or satisfying a case of wanderlust. As avid outdoor devotees and advocates of wise use, we stress the importance of treading lightly in our favorite areas, so they remain healthy and welcome us back for years to come. It is always recess in Colorado's playground. Come wander in circles with us.

Trail Etiquette

What better way to wander the land than a good hike? Tuck your feet into a faithful pair of boots, find a favorite trail, and just go. Sure, hiking gets us out there in a wonderful, uninhibited escape, but we still need to use our noggins to share the outdoor experience. A little common sense and old-fashioned courtesy go a long way to assure a good time for everyone. Chances are good that you will cross paths with other user groups, like mountain bikers, horseback riders, trail runners, or folks hiking with dogs. All of us need to recreate responsibly with a keen respect for the environment to preserve the trails we enjoy so much, especially in the backcountry.

When meeting other hikers, those traveling uphill have the right of way. The ascending hiker is often focused on the trail immediately ahead to scan for obstacles or maintain a steady pace, and might not even see a downhill group until they nearly bonk heads. It is also easier for descending hikers to rein in their strides and give the uphill group room to keep on truckin'. Horseback riders have the right of way all the time, regardless of the type of user. Hikers should exit the trail, on the downhill side if possible, to avoid intimidating the horses. Talk to the riders as they pass and

Mountain Park Environmental Bus

don't stand behind trees or other concealing foliage; a spooked horse can instantly switch gears from a leisurely clip-clop to a full-out, homestretch sprint. Being more mobile, hikers can easily yield to trail runners and mountain bikers, as well, both of whom rapidly overtake our slower footsteps. While traditional practice sees bikes yield to boots, it is often wiser to step off trail to let cyclists pass, instead of the bikers riding around you or having to dismount and get their own steeds out of the way.

Along with good manners, we should also remember to tread lightly in our travels and practice minimum impact. Check out some suggestions in the Leave No Trace section later in this Introduction.

CAMPING

Ambling along a trail in the wilderness, with crystal skies and cool mountain air—not much else could make it better, except one thing: staying longer. Most of the hikes in this book are day trips, from a quick couple of hours to a 14-hour trek, but nearly every one of them has opportunities for camping. The multiday hikes are ideal for extended backpacking trips. Throwing down a tent in perfect solitude gives us a seamless outdoor experience, and can add a whole new page of memories. Seeing as how we are sensible outdoor enthusiasts, we use our tread-lightly habits from the trail at the campsite, too. Low-impact camping has all kinds of benefits—for us, for other users, for the local flora and fauna, and especially for the land itself. Here are a few handy tips:

- Use an established tent site whenever available. These sites position campers in areas least likely to trample fragile vegetation or cause erosion. If no site is available, choose an area with rocky or sandy soil.
- When it comes to personal business, backcountry bathroom efforts require slight changes in your usual routine. If there is an outhouse in the vicinity, make use of it. An outdoor loo is there to keep nature tidy and clean. If no toilet is available, head far from the campsite and any creeks, trails, or lakes, dig a hole 6–8 inches deep, and do your thing. When finished, bury the waste with the previously removed dirt and cover with leaves and sticks.
- Resist the urge to build a campfire. In many areas of Colorado, campfires are not allowed for several reasons, the obvious one being to prevent starting a devastating forest fire. Frequent scavenge hunts for firewood eventually denude the area of downfall, which serves as food and habitat for a lot of little critters. Bring a camp stove and save the fires for parks with designated pits.
- Hold fast to the "pack it in, pack it out" edict. Everything you bring should stay with you for the entire trip and all the way back to the trailhead (except the stuff buried in the hole).

LEAVE NO TRACE

Our reminders about treating the land with care are largely derived from the longstanding Leave No Trace principles developed in the '70s. Used far and

Flat Tops in northern Colorado

wide today in both teaching and practice, the goal of these seven tenets is to educate outdoor visitors about the effect of their recreational impacts and to offer suggestions on how to minimize those impacts. Here they are:

1. **Plan ahead and prepare.** A little forethought and advance planning on what you are getting yourself into will ensure an enjoyable and trouble-free trip. Pack gear appropriate to your destination; don't head up to 14,000 feet in a tee shirt and flip-flops. Expect emergencies and carry supplies to deal with them, like first-aid kits and repair material for broken packs. Carry a map and a compass and know how to use them. Bring extra batteries for GPS units and headlamps.

2. **Travel and camp on durable surfaces.** Hike on designated trails and never cut switchbacks. Stay on the trail or stay home. Social trails and shortcuts cause erosion and destroy the integrity of the land. Don't tromp through sensitive riparian areas. Camp at least 200 feet from lakes and streams to ensure little to no impact on water sources. In remote wilderness, disperse use to minimize impact.

3. **Dispose of waste properly.** Pack it in, pack it out. All trash, extra food, even toilet paper needs to return with you at trip's end. Use warm water

to wash yourself and dishes, and do so the aforementioned 200 feet from water sources. Use only small amounts of biodegradable soap.

4. **Leave what you find.** Observe and enjoy historic and cultural sights, but do so from a distance that will preserve them as they are. Leave the natural world—plants, rocks, streams—as you found it. Do not remove anything from the wild. Remember the familiar motto, "leave only footprints."

5. **Minimize campfire impacts.** Campfires cause long-lasting impacts to the backcountry. Cook with a camp stove and wear proper gear to stay warm. If fires are permitted where you travel, use established fire pits or rings and keep the fire small. Burn fires completely out, until ashes are cool, and scatter ashes before leaving the site.

6. **Respect wildlife.** Observe wildlife from a respectable distance, and do not approach them. While it is tempting to move in just a little closer, your actions are likely to frighten the animals, or at the very least greatly annoy them. An agitated moose, for example, could put all sorts of hurt on an unwanted intruder. Enjoy the animals' habitat with the appreciation and respect of a visitor because, after all, that is what we are.

7. **Be considerate of other visitors.** Common courtesy goes a long way, even way out in the woods. Respect other users to ensure a quality experience for everyone. Yield to horses at all times and to mountain bikes where appropriate. Encourage solitude by camping away from other users. Be quiet and just listen to the land.

WEATHER

Colorado's weather is impressively unpredictable and hikers need to be prepared for sudden changes at any time of the year. In the high mountains, temperatures can plummet 20 degrees faster than you can say, "Uh-oh, I forgot my jacket." Rainsqualls can develop in short order, too, and hypothermia is all but assured if you are caught unaware. Altitude sickness can sneak up on hikers unaccustomed to higher elevations. Intense heat in the desert areas of the state, even in seemingly innocent locations along the Front Range, can rapidly roast you and make you look like an embarrassed lobster. Snow can fall in the mountains any time of the year—in copious amounts and often when least expected, like on a carefree mid-August afternoon. Thunderstorms are probably the biggest concern because with them comes lightning. Storms of various intensities occur almost every afternoon in the summer months, sometimes as a refreshing mist that is over in minutes, other times in a violent deluge that keeps you tent-bound for days. Other times there may be no rain at all, just clouds and lightning, and that spells trouble. Lightning strikes are scary to a hiker wandering across an exposed ridge, and they can be deadly. Here are a few things you can do to be ready for lightning and, most of all, stay alive out there:

■ **Be prepared.** Always check the weather before a trip and make sure to get early starts. If you are climbing a high peak, plan to get off the summit by noon and out of exposure by early afternoon.

- **Be studious.** Listen for thunder and study the clouds above. Typically, cumulonimbus clouds are the cause of dangerous thunderstorms. Look for these large, puffy clouds that grow vertically into anvil shapes.
- **Don't forget the 5-second rule.** When you see a flash of lightning, count the seconds until you hear thunder. Dividing the number of seconds by five will tell you how many miles away the storm is. Although rare, rogue lightning bolts can strike miles away from actual rain areas, so always stay alert.
- **Move to safety.** If you cannot avoid a storm, get off peaks and ridges quickly, move into the shadow of a mountain, and avoid shelter under trees (unless in a heavily forested area where trees are uniform in height), near water, under rocks, and in caves.
- **Assume lightning position.** If you can feel your skin tingle, and your hair is standing on edge, lightning is imminent. When caught in a storm, crouch down into lightning position. Put your weight on the balls of your feet and touch your heels together. Rest your elbows on your knees and lace your fingers over your head. This position creates little surface

Watch for sled dogs at Camp Hale.

with the ground to avoid ground currents and provides an electrical path through your body to avoid your head and heart. Try to stand on some kind of insulator, such as a backpack, sleep pad, dirt, or grass. Disperse the group. When hiking in groups, don't forget that one bolt of lightning can strike more than one person. Space yourselves a considerable distance so survivors can revive victims if needed.

AVALANCHES

Avalanches in Colorado claim lives every year, and they are a threat year-round in many areas of the state. Deep snowfields can remain even in the heat of summer and can break loose and slide with no warning. In a race with a mountain of snow hurtling downhill at 100+ mph, you will lose. At best, it will scare the bejeezus out of you. If you travel in the backcountry, use your head to stay out of trouble.

- **Be prepared.** Check the weather and call rangers to ask about snow conditions. If you know you'll be traveling where avalanche is a possibility, carry beacons, shovels, and poles. Don't travel alone. Cross danger zones one person at a time. Take an avalanche safety course.
- **Be studious.** Most avalanches occur on hillsides with a 30-degree slope or steeper. Danger is highest during or immediately following storms.
- **Move with the slide.** If you're caught in an avalanche, try to "swim" with it in order to stay on top. Make every effort to move to the side of the avalanche. When the slide begins to stop, cover your face and create airspace. Do your best not to panic: excessive breathing can melt snow and create an airtight ice shield.

WILDLIFE

We are fortunate to live in a state still rich with wildlife. But the state is popular with humans, too, and more people take up more room, causing wildlife habitat to disappear. This pattern has caused more and more human-wildlife interaction in recent years, with many of those meetings of the negative variety. It is important to remember that an animal's first choice is not to attack you, but when they are with their offspring or feel threatened they will put up a ferocious fight to protect themselves and their young. If and when you encounter wildlife, stay calm and give them plenty of room to vamoose. Don't hike alone, and never let your children run ahead or linger behind. With some simple precautions, unexpected engagements with critters can be an exciting privilege rather than a frightening experience.

Bears

The only species of bear found in Colorado is the black bear (although there is often speculation and excitement that a grizzly or two might be out there). Typically, a bear will be alerted to your presence and lumber away before you can make contact. Bears love an easy meal, so keep a clean camp, don't

Bighorns just above tree line on the Triple Threat loop

bury trash, and if camping, hang food at least 10 feet high and 4 feet out from a tree trunk. If you do encounter a bear, remember these tips:

- **Remain calm.** A bear will usually only attack if threatened. If the bear hasn't seen you, calmly leave the area.
- **Stop hiking.** If a bear has seen you, back away slowly. Don't make eye contact (it may perceive this as a threat) and talk quietly. Do not run or climb a tree. These actions may provoke a predatory reaction and you won't be able to outrun or outclimb a bear.
- **Fight back.** People can and have fended off black bears with rocks, sticks, water bottles, etc.

Mountain lions

These elusive animals are being pushed out of their habitat at alarming rates; chances are, mountain homeowners will see these big cats more frequently than hikers. If you are lucky enough to see a mountain lion:

- **Remain calm and stop hiking.** Like a bear, running away may trigger a natural desire to chase and attack.
- **Appear as large as possible.** Show that cat who is boss. Open up your

jacket, stand tall, and wave your arms. Shout at the animal and throw rocks and sticks to scare it away. Avoid eye contact.

■ **Fight back.** Just as with bears, people have successfully warded off lions by using anything available, including bare hands.

Of course, Colorado's animal world is not just populated by large beasts like bears, mountain lions, and moose. You are likely to see many other species of the wildlife while out on the trails, like marmots, wild turkeys, rattlers, ptarmigan, pikas, foxes, bobcats, and more.

GEAR

Wearing and carrying proper equipment is essential before venturing out on any hike. A short stroll on local park trails requires less in the way of survival gear than a weeklong alpine journey, but you still need to bring the right stuff. Technical gear for hiking and packing is widely available, affordable, comfortable, and lets you enjoy the hike without fussing with uncooperative equipment.

Keeping your body relaxed and cozy is most important, and synthetic clothing is the way to go. It wicks moisture to keep you cool when it's hot and provides a barrier to biting cold. Leave your cotton duds at home; cotton is a poor insulator and is miserable to wear when wet. Wear layers to adjust to changing conditions; that heavy thermal expedition parka will be mighty steamy when the sun sends temperatures sizzling. Your feet are probably the most critical item to take care of. Start with a comfy pair of socks, and cover them with the best pair of hiking boots you can find. A collection of festering blisters 10 miles into a hike is a sure way to have you questioning your choice of activities. Happy feet will make your trek one to remember.

On longer hikes, there are several indispensable items you need to have along. The biggies are a quality, lightweight sleeping bag and pad, camp stove, plenty of food, and of course a good pack to carry it all. But there are many other supplies to consider to ease your mind and ensure safety in the wilderness. The Ten Essentials is a list of items that you should always have in your pack:

1. **Navigation (map and compass).** Know how to use them, as well. A compass can guide you out of dense woods or featureless landscapes.
2. **Nutrition (extra food).** Bring enough to keep fueled in case of emergencies.
3. **Hydration (extra water).** Bring enough water, too, and drink before you're thirsty. Dehydration happens in a hurry at high altitudes. Carry a water filter to supplement what you can't carry.
4. **Insulation (extra clothing).** Expect the worst weather and prepare for it with gear like a rain jacket, hat, and extra socks.
5. **Repair kit and tools (including a knife).** A good knife serves many purposes, and a multitool is even better, for repairing damaged stoves or packs, whittling off wood for kindling, cutting rope, etc.
6. **First-aid supplies.** Be ready for emergencies. Even a minor cut or

Poison Ivy

abrasion can create problems if left untreated. Carry bandages, gauze, moleskin, aspirin, and the like. A first-aid training course can also come in handy.

7. **Fire (firestarter and matches/lighter).** Use the strike-anywhere type or waterproof matches, and put them in a waterproof container. This is one of your most important survival tools, as a warm fire can get you through a cold night or cook food in case of a damaged stove. A critical complement to matches, firestarter is essential for providing a fire in unfavorable conditions. Carry some in your pack and also in a separate waterproof case in your pocket.

8. **Illumination (flashlight or headlamp).** If you are lost in the black of night, these tools will help you find your way. Also bring extra batteries and bulbs.

9. **Sun protection (sunglasses and sunscreen).** Good sunglasses are crucial for outdoor travel, especially at high altitudes. Sunscreen will keep your skin cooler and help prevent heatstroke.

10. **Emergency shelter.** All the goodies above won't help much if you are stuck outside in the snow or rain. Protection is the best way to survive such troubling dilemmas. A sure-fire solution is a lightweight, nylon poncho or tarp and nylon cord. Add to this a featherweight space

blanket to ensure a dry floor, and you can set up an emergency refuge in no time.

There are a few additional items that should also be added to the list, especially if you are planning an extended trip:

Insect repellant. Many glorious mountain excursions have been blemished by bugs. Sometimes it's like a plague of locusts o'er the land—there is no escape from the miserable little pests. You can make life a bit easier by loading up on bug repellant. The most effective types are DEET-based, but there are numerous other options as well. Or wear bug-resistant clothing; loose-fitting pants and long-sleeve shirts, or even bug-net hats, put up a good defense.

Water purifier. A shimmering stream gurgles near the trail. The water is cold and looks pure as the driven snow. Just one little drink won't hurt, right? Better think twice, pardner. Germs and viruses are alive and well even in the deepest wilderness, and they are especially prevalent in lakes and streams. That means purifying all water before taking a big swig. It takes a few extra minutes, but just ask anyone who has acquired *Giardia* whether it is worth the time to filter. Symptoms of these ubiquitous protozoa include, but are not limited to, diarrhea, flatulence, bloating, vomiting, and fever. Lots

Trailside flowers

of unpleasant nastiness, none of which you would like to have along on your trip, or back home with the family. Don't drink water straight out of rivers, lakes, or streams, no matter how clean and tasty they may appear. A few simple methods and products can be used to combat waterborne bacteria:

- **Boiling.** Most bacteria are killed as soon as water comes to a full boil, but a few minutes of boiling will kill germs and viruses alike. While this method is effective, it uses up a lot of stove fuel; plan accordingly.
- **Iodine.** Iodine can be purchased at most outdoor shops and comes in liquid and tablet form. Generally, eight drops per quart of water are needed to sufficiently kill any bacterium.
- **Purifiers and filters.** Packable water filtration systems have become widely popular for their ease and efficiency in use. Just drop in a tube and fill a bottle of cool, fresh H2O. Check specific models for their capacities and uses.

USING THIS BOOK

Each hike in the book begins with an information block to orient you to the highlights of the trail. We use the following categories to provide this initial introduction:

- **Round trip.** This is the total mileage for the trip. GPS navigation was used for the majority of the hikes to get the most accurate distances possible.
- **Loop direction.** As each hike is a loop, there are only two directions in which to hike them: clockwise or counterclockwise. While some directions were picked arbitrarily, we tried to hike in the direction most befitting to the scenery of each trail, and what we thought would be the best physically.
- **Hiking time.** One of the authors of this book is a marathoner, the other a competitive cyclist, and we both have an insatiable hunger to push our limits. As a result, our hiking times may be different than yours, but we tried to calculate times we think are reasonable to enjoy the hike with plenty of stops for food, water, and general gawking at the gorgeous scenery.
- **Sweat factor.** This is our term for "difficulty level." We rate the trails as easy, moderate, or difficult, and consider factors such as distance, elevation gain, terrain, and the like. A plus sign is added as necessary to bump up the rating.
- **Starting elevation, high point, low point, elevation gain.** These numbers let you know how much climbing will be involved. We've included everything from short, flat trails to long, fourteener routes to give you options based on your ability.
- **Best hiking season.** This can be a subjective category. None of the hikes emphasize winter conditions, although some can be accessed by snowshoes and are quite beautiful under a fresh blanket of snow. Generally, we thought the best times of year were in midspring, when the wildflowers are at their best, and midfall, when Colorado's famous aspens are ablaze.

Opposite: Profile Rock on the Pollock Bench Trail

Long, winding bench above the Colorado River

- **Maps.** We note available USGS quads for each trail, along with any additional maps we might have used. Route maps shown in this book are for reference only; do not depend on them to save your hide from navigational debacles. Utilize an up-to-date map you are comfortable with, and know how to use it. Elevation profiles are also provided, but only as reference. The trails are not typically as difficult as some profiles appear.
- **Contact.** We have listed the various organizations responsible for maintenance and information regarding the areas we will be hiking. These are great resources to check the weather for an area, ask questions concerning regulations, and obtain any other details you may want before heading out. Resource contact information is listed in the appendix.
- **Driving directions.** Easy-to-follow directions to the trailhead.

After the information block is a general introduction and a narrative description of each trail with trail names, signs and intersections, flora and fauna along the way, interesting and historical facts that may characterize the area, and good rest stops. We had an unforgettable season exploring Colorado's finest, and we hope this book helps you do the same.

A NOTE ABOUT SAFETY

Safety is an important concern in all outdoor activities. No guidebook can alert you to every hazard or anticipate the limitations of every reader. Therefore, the descriptions of roads, trails, routes, and natural features in this book are not representations that a particular place or excursion will be safe for your party. When you follow any of the routes described in this book, you assume responsibility for your own safety. Under normal conditions, such excursions require the usual attention to traffic, road and trail conditions, weather, terrain, the capabilities of your party, and other factors. Keeping informed on current conditions and exercising common sense are the keys to a safe, enjoyable outing.

—The Mountaineers Books

HIKES BY INTEREST
(NOT ALL HIKES ARE LISTED; SOME ARE LISTED TWICE)

Easy Strolls	Challenging Treks	Kid Friendly	Overnighters	Fourteeners (on the hike or nearby)
Hike Number and Name				
3. Dowdy Lake	32. Fancy Pass Trail	3. Dowdy Lake	16. Devils Thumb	33. Mount of the Holy Cross
6. ELC Loop	33. Mount of the Holy Cross	6. ELC Loop	48. Wall Lake Loop	34. Four Score
17. Barr Lake State Park	34. Four Score	7. Devils Backbone Trail	52. Little Matterhorn	36. Crater Lake Trail
23. Garden of the Gods	48. Wall Lake Loop	8. Eagle Wind Trail		40. Storms Gulch Trail
31. Petrified Forest Loop	51. Triple Threat	17. Barr Lake State Park		41. Jud Wiebe Trail
44. Oak Flat Loop	52. Little Matterhorn	23. Garden of the Gods		42. Wilson Mesa Loop
		31. Petrified Forest Loop		43. Portland Trail
		44. Oak Flat Loop		50. Gem Lake Loop
		60. Sprague Lake Loop		51. Triple Threat

FRONT RANGE AND VICINITY

1 MOUNT McCONNEL TRAIL

Round trip	**4.3 miles**
Loop direction	Clockwise
Hiking time	2.5 to 3 hours
Sweat factor	Moderate
Starting elevation	6743 feet
High point	8000 feet
Low point	6547 feet
Elevation gain	1256 feet
Best hiking season	April through November
Maps	USGS Big Narrows
Contact	Roosevelt National Forest

Driving directions: To reach the trailhead from Fort Collins, drive north on US 287 to Ted's Place and Colorado 14 at the mouth of Poudre Canyon. Follow the canyon road 24 miles to the Mountain Park campground and take a left across the bridge. Go right at the first junction toward the day-use trailhead and picnic areas. The trailhead is on the left.

Legend has it that in 1820 a number of French fur trappers were caught in a terrific snowstorm in northern Colorado. It was vital to drop everything but the bare essentials in order to survive. Rather than waste their gunpowder, the trappers decided to bury it near the river bordering their travel route. That river is now known as the Cache la Poudre, or "hiding place of powder." The high canyon walls and rolling forests of this area attracted Native Americans, trappers, miners, and timber crews. Today the Poudre Canyon draws adventurers of a different breed to hike, fish, raft, or camp. The Mount McConnel Trail in the Cache la Poudre Wilderness Area delivers terrific views of the northern reaches of the Mummy Range and of the canyon and its namesake river below. The path switchbacks all the way up to the summit and follows a steep and challenging descent back to the beginning of this short loop.

From the lower parking area, the

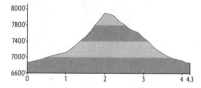

trail winds left from the trailhead sign, crosses the road leading to the upper parking area and passes another informational kiosk. This trail is one of only two maintained trails, leading to the only named peak in the whole of this second smallest wilderness area in the state. Let's take advantage and head south on this rocky trail up into a grove of ponderosa, Douglas-fir, and juniper. The path switchbacks rather steeply and passes a number of informational signs providing information concerning our immediate surroundings, including elevations and zone charts, forest management, and fauna and foliage of the area.

Passing through the official boundaries of the wilderness area, the trail gets rockier, bitterbrush moves in around our ankles, and traces of mountain mahogany reach for our shoulders. We are quickly gaining ground here, and there are great views of the curling Poudre River rushing through the granite bedrock canyon far below. Look for big bends in the river that create deep pools and eddies; on brilliant summer days you can see heads and hats of fly-fishers casting for a variety of species of trout. The Poudre is Colorado's only National Wild and Scenic River, and the fishing is fine indeed. The trail continues its series of steep switchbacks and reaches a junction with the Kreutzer Trail at 0.6 mile. On an interesting side note, William Kreutzer, at the young age of 20, was the first official forest ranger in the United States back in 1898 at the Plum Creek Timberland Reserve in central Colorado.

Here a decision needs to be made. Either branch makes for an arduous loop, but let's head left on the Mount McConnel Trail. We traverse back to the east along a ridge that exposes views above the rolling hills of the Poudre

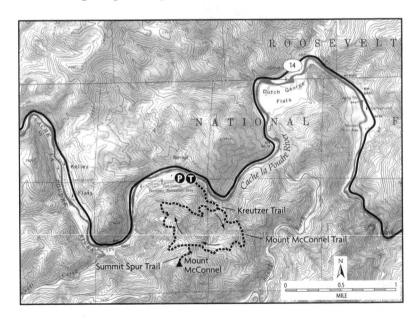

Summit of Mount McConnel

Canyon out to the eastern plains, and cruise back south into the trees toward the next junction. At 1.8 miles, let's break off to the left toward the Summit Spur Trail to access the high point of this beautiful hike. A short, 0.15-mile jaunt past a small ridge of wind-protecting rocks brings us to a final out-cropping marking the summit of Mount McConnel. A number of nooks and crannies provide shelter from the wind to rest and enjoy the views of the wil-derness. After a quick break, we head back down through the ponderosas to rejoin the Mount McConnel Trail and continue heading east. Before any real sign of descent, the sandy trail undulates along the top edge of the mountain and travels through a landscape pocked by gnarled snag trees, broad flat stones, and a huge rock bench. A tilt in the land pulls us down along a squirrelly trail ducking under fir trees, hopping over rocks, and making tight little switchbacks on a well-maintained trail. The path wraps farther west back toward the start of the hike, and this north-facing hillside takes the shape of a huge, steep amphitheatre. At 3.6 miles, we arrive at the other end of the Kreutzer Trail. Let's stay left to make our way back to the beginning of the hike, now with the accompaniment of interpretative signs. Finally, the trail follows a more manageable grade along a mellow contour. The roar of the Cache la Poudre River comes into earshot and we parallel the water back to the entrance road for the campground and trailhead.

2 | GREYROCK TRAIL

Round trip ■	**6.5 miles**
Loop direction ■	Clockwise
Hiking time ■	3 to 4 hours
Sweat factor ■	Moderate+
Starting elevation ■	5577 feet
High point ■	7540 feet
Low point ■	5510 feet
Elevation gain ■	2694 feet
Best hiking season ■	Year-round
Maps ■	USGS Poudre Park
Contact ■	Roosevelt National Forest

Driving directions: Follow US 287 northwest from Fort Collins to Colorado 14, then head up the canyon 8 miles to the trailhead. Signs are posted and there is parking on the south side of the road for a few dozen cars. This is a popular trail and the lot fills quickly on weekends. Plan accordingly. The hike begins on the north side of the highway.

Greyrock Mountain is a big ol' granite dome above Poudre Canyon, and the fun loop trail to the summit makes a great day hike. The hike travels over well-maintained tread to a peaceful meadow, then up and over some huge

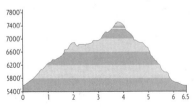

boulders to the summit and great views to the east. The trail starts in the lower reaches of the ruggedly scenic Poudre Canyon, and crosses right over the Cache la Poudre River. The river offers fantastic fishing and whitewater rafting, and

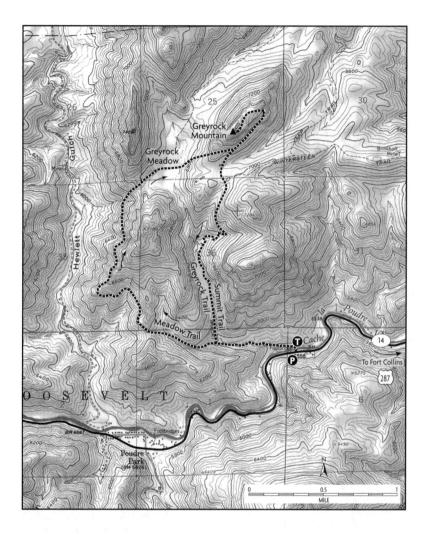

many campsites along its banks provide opportunity for extended stays in the canyon.

The first steps on this hike lead to a long wooden bridge reaching across the river. In the spring, the water's rapids roil and this is the perfect place to watch bulbous rubber rafts ride the frothy current with excited hoots and hollers from would-be skippers. The Poudre is a lively river for rafting, and its quiet bends and pools also provide some of the best trout fishing in the state. After the bridge crossing, the gravel path gently ascends west, paralleling the road and the river through stands of ponderosa pine. Keep an eye on the ground on the way up for poison ivy sprouting in abundance. Our path generally follows this drainage to a junction at 0.6 mile. The loop starts here, with the Summit Trail heading north toward the mountain, and the Meadow Trail leading west up a narrow valley. Let's choose the Meadow Trail, continuing on a steady ascent through the drainage's damp corridor of foliage. The trail becomes steep enough for some switchbacks, and as we approach 1 mile, the trail heads out of the trees onto the hot south-facing side of this valley. We soon begin a northwesterly ascent up a huge sage-covered hill dotted with ponderosa, juniper, and boulders of various sizes. The trail continues northwest and enters the seam of a gulch, which climbs steadily in elevation, then switchbacks out of the gulch at 1.6 miles, where it breaches a ridge with fine views east of the Poudre Canyon and rolling mountains to the west. The path then climbs to another ridge, angling northeast through an ample collection of broken rock. At 2 miles, a gap in the mountains to the east opens up to great views of Fort Collins and the plains beyond. Just ahead, over the crest of this ridge, is our first glimpse of Greyrock Mountain. From here, we'll descend onto a slope of ponderosa, fir, and juniper on our way down to the valley nestled below.

The trail bottoms out and heads east on the southern fringe of this beautiful open meadow with fantastic views of Greyrock. The meadow seems out of place up here, but its tall grasses and solitary groves of ponderosa are a treat in the midst of the hard mood of so much rock. Hugging the southern edge of the valley, we will cross a small drainage approaching mile 3 and exit the valley, beginning the initial ascent toward the apex of the hike. Follow the trail up a few terraces of trees and rocks and through a small burned area

Hidden pond on top of Greyrock Mountain (Photo by Sierra Overlie)

to the base of the mountain. A junction here splits the trail into the return portion of the loop and the Summit Trail. Let's head to the top, climbing over and around huge boulders. The path becomes faint and even difficult to find in places, but a series of cairns leads the way.

Greyrock's summit rewards us with a hidden pond tucked among monstrous boulders and panoramic views of the high plains to the east and mountains in the other three directions. This peak is a great place to hang out, with secluded copses and fun jumbles of rocks to clamber on or just perch and gaze at the horizon, with a chorus of frogs in the pond for background music. After loitering up top, we follow the same path back down to the junction and hang a left to finish the second half of the loop. The trail immediately heads south and drops into a deep gulch loaded with ponderosa, then undulates up and down with nice views of the Poudre River all the while.

We will switchback down open hillsides and corridors of woods, hiking on a tread of rocks and roots to the bottom of the gulch and a small stream. The path leads southeast through lush undergrowth and gets a bit steep and rocky at times, so use caution. In just a short while we have made it back to the first junction and completion of the loop. A left turn here and an easy half-mile brings us back to the bridge and the trailhead. A great hike, indeed, and still plenty of time for a riverside picnic or a visit back to town for refreshments.

3 DOWDY LAKE

Round trip ■	**2.2 miles**
Loop direction ■	Clockwise
Hiking time ■	1 hour
Sweat factor ■	Low
Starting elevation ■	8127 feet
High point ■	8176 feet
Low point ■	8127 feet
Elevation gain ■	51 feet
Best hiking season ■	April through October
Maps ■	USGS Red Feather Lakes
Contact ■	Roosevelt National Forest

Driving directions: To reach Dowdy Lake from Fort Collins, drive 24 miles north on Highway 287 to Livermore and follow County Road 74 west for 24 more miles. Turn north onto Forest Road 218 and proceed 0.75 mile past the campsite to the northern side of the lake.

Long summer days in Colorado are made to order for outdoor enthusiasts, with a lot of sun and reliable weather for exploring our favorite hideaways. And the lingering evenings entertain us with warm, colorful sunsets on a sky that reaches into forever. Dowdy Lake is the perfect location to absorb such evenings. Tucked away in northern Colorado, Dowdy is the biggest of a handful of lakes known as the Red Feather Lakes. This is a great family destination with camping, fishing, hiking, canoeing, bird-watching, and picnic grounds. Whether you're strolling in and out of ponderosas, floating gently past the chimney rock formations jutting from the lake, or setting up camp beneath the aspen leaves, the Red Feather area is a Colorado gem.

Let's start this short stroll at the northernmost point of the lake and saunter south along the eastern shore. Tall grasses wave in the wind and are freckled with the occasional ponderosa pine and intriguing pillars of rock. The trail grows faint at times and is riddled with social trails, but as long as we follow the lakeshore we'll be sure to complete the loop. Long views of the area dominated by ponderosa wander out of sight in nearly all directions.

Around half a mile in, we cruise past the first of a few beaches perfect for enjoying breakfast or dinner and sprawling out to relax. Depending on

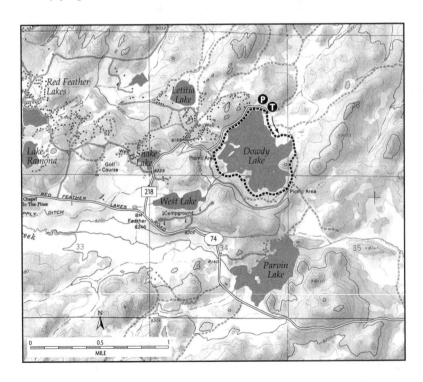

Dowdy Lake

the condition and direction of the wind, these beaches are also an excellent area for anglers. The stocked lake features a variety of fish, including native cutthroat, rainbow, brown, and brook trout, and Kokanee salmon. From here, the trail winds in and out of trees as it traces fingers of water jutting into the shoreline.

As the trail wraps around the southern end of the lake, it passes an outcropping of rocks, sneaks over the boat ramp, and arrives back at the trailhead.

4 ARTHURS ROCK

Round trip ■	**5.9 miles**
Loop direction ■	Counterclockwise
Hiking time ■	5 hours
Sweat factor ■	Moderate
Starting elevation ■	5520 feet
High point ■	6780 feet
Low point ■	5520 feet
Elevation gain ■	2439 feet
Best hiking season ■	April through October
Maps ■	USGS Horsetooth Reservoir; Lory State Park
Contact ■	Colorado State Parks, Lory

Driving directions: To reach the park from Fort Collins, go to the west edge of town and follow Overland Trail north to Bingham Hill Road (County 50E). Head up over the hill to a left turn at County 23N. Follow 23 south to County 25G, just before reaching the north dam of

Horsetooth Reservoir, and turn right. This road climbs over a hogback, past a small residential area, and dead-ends at the park entrance. Stop at the visitor center and pony up the $5 entrance fee, then follow the gravel road to the Eltuck Picnic Area on the left. The trailhead for the Well Gulch Nature Trail is right across the road.

This is an excellent hike in Lory State Park in the foothills west of Fort Collins. Lory, one of forty Colorado state parks, includes more than 2400 acres of diverse terrain providing 20 miles of trails for hiking, mountain biking, and horseback riding. This hike explores a scenic gulch, climbs through mountain meadows, and brings us up high to Arthurs Rock, with breathtaking views of Horsetooth Reservoir, Fort Collins below, and the expanse of the eastern plains beyond.

Our hike begins on a hard-packed gravel path leading west past low shrubs toward the gulch. At the base of the gulch is a short bridge crossing a skinny creek and a junction with a sign for Timber Trail and Arthurs Rock. Let's go that way (right), following a gentle uphill grade along the creek into a narrow canyon. The trail crosses the creek above a petite waterfall and becomes rockier as it continues to climb. This is a beautiful canyon, with ponderosa pine, Douglas-fir, and spruce mixed in with huge round boulders. A high rock wall rises at our left shoulder, casting almost perpetual shade on this part of the trail. After a couple more creek crossings, the trail makes two sweeping switchbacks and emerges into a meadow setting in a stand of giant ponderosas. Look over there! There goes a trio of wild turkeys, sprinting into the tall grasses and shrubbery. Keep your eyes peeled for other wildlife on this hike, too, like mule deer and maybe even a mountain lion.

A half-mile into the hike, we reach the split with the return segment of the Well Gulch Nature Trail. The Timber Trail to the right leads to Arthurs Rock, so we will continue climbing away from the drainage up the north slope of the canyon on hard-packed, relatively rock-free tread. Look back down to the east for a great view of Horsetooth Reservoir and Fort Collins beyond. Overhead, raptors soar on the mountain winds near the rock formations far above. Our path contours along the hill in a southwesterly direction, straight into the clutches of a dense wood. At a curve in the path, a beauteous view appears of the reservoir way down below. Horsetooth is a major player in the Colorado–Big Thompson water supply project, diverting water from the Western Slope through tunnels and canals to Front Range cities and farms on the eastern plains.

After another short climb, the trail begins to level and we enjoy easy walking to the 2-mile mark. This junction means a left turn for us onto the wide access road, coasting downhill for a short distance, then turning back up again. As we near the hike's high point, more and more long-distance

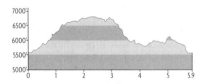

views reveal themselves through the trees and from rock outcroppings along the trail. A junction at 2.7 miles indicates the Arthurs Rock trailhead (downhill to the right) and the Arthurs Rock summit (uphill to the left). The last

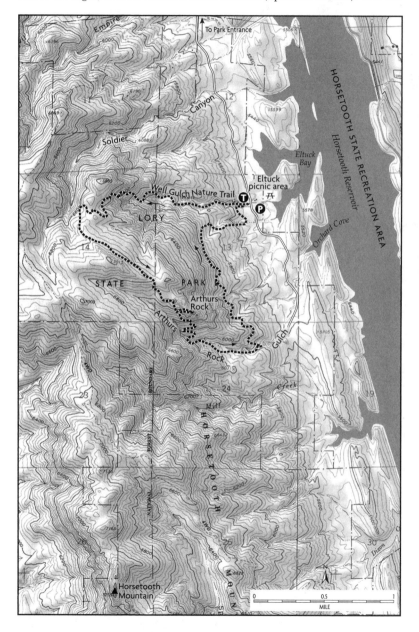

Early trail to Authurs Rock

grind to the top is a scramble over and around huge boulders on the backside of the peak, until we finally plant our boots on Arthurs' lumpy, rounded summit. A couple of dozen ponderosa have taken residence up here, and some of the hardiest grow right out of the rock itself. The higher jumble of rocks to the south offers a great spot to rest and soak in the far-reaching views of the eastern plains. Along the west shores of the reservoir, look for the long ridgeline running the entire length of the reservoir and even farther to the south. Pretty impressive display of geologic handiwork, eh? Check out the miniature craters in the top of this rock—pint-size birdbaths after a good rain.

Time to head down. After carefully negotiating the descent from Arthurs Rock, take a left at the sign for Arthurs Rock Trail. The path turns back to the east, passing next to the colossal south face of Arthurs. A few gentle switchbacks bring us into an open area of grasses and low shrubs. We are close to another drainage on this section of the hike, but this one has not even a trickle of water. At a curve in the trail, nearly clear of the drainage and into open territory, we're going to leave the main route and head left on a narrow footpath. The plan is to work our way back north to Eltuck Bay on a more scenic path.

This part of the trail might invoke much protesting from tired legs. The trail climbs steeply for a long way, through a fold in the hill and up over a huge hummock, back down into a second crinkle in the landscape, and uphill yet again, until finally settling in to a manageable rhythm all the way to the end of the hike. At the junction with the Well Gulch Nature Trail, let's turn right and follow the path toward the reservoir. Right before the parking lot at the Homestead Picnic Area, we'll take one more left turn and stroll among tall grasses back to the first bridge crossing and down to the trailhead.

5 HORSETOOTH MOUNTAIN TRAIL

Round trip ■	**4.5 miles**
Loop direction ■	Counterclockwise
Hiking time ■	3 hours
Sweat factor ■	Moderate
Starting elevation ■	5753 feet
High point ■	7255 feet
Low point ■	5753 feet
Elevation gain ■	1392
Best hiking season ■	April through November
Maps ■	USGS Horsetooth Reservoir
Contact ■	Larimer County Parks and Recreation

Driving directions: To reach the trailhead from Fort Collins, follow Harmony Road west toward the mountains. At Taft Hill Road, Harmony Road becomes County Road 38E. Follow this road for 6 miles into the foothills and around Horsetooth Reservoir, through Stout, Colorado (population 47½ according to the locals), to the trailhead parking lot on top of the hill above Stout. Permits are required for everyone entering the park (including walk-ins and bike-ins) and cost $6. Fees go to Larimer County Parks to keep these parks in top shape.

Just 5 of the 28 miles nestled in Horsetooth Mountain Park, this lollipop trail offers wonderful views of much of Colorado's dynamic landscape. It is a great place to bring the family; the entire park encompasses 2500 acres of land and is accessible for hikers, bikers, and horses. Perched at over 7000 feet, Horsetooth Mountain is a familiar symbol for those dwelling in nearby Fort Collins. This hike climbs steadily through forested hogbacks right up to the rock, with long-distance views of the towns below and the high plains to the east.

Here, we go up a few switchbacks into the woods and now the trail parallels a small creek on the left and a cluster of large, handsome boulders on the right. All the while we are treated to the sights and smells characterizing the Rocky Mountains—the vanilla fragrance of the ponderosas and semisweet twinge of sage during hot, arid summers; the sounds of wind in the trees and melodic tunes of meadowlarks and other songbirds. Another sound we might hear is the crunch of gravel beneath the knobby tires of a mountain bike barreling down the hill at high velocity. This trail is open to bikes, too, so stay alert for unexpected company.

Our path banks hard to the right

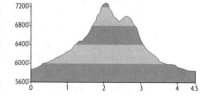

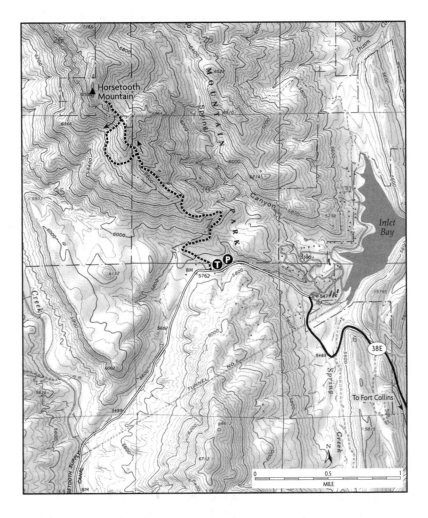

and ascends some wooden steps leading up through the boulders. At the top, a rocky platform affords a beautiful view of Fort Collins and the eastern banks of Horsetooth Reservoir. A little more zigzagging and we arrive at a four-way intersection; cruise straight through, and climb to a plateau with a peek at the southeast side of Horsetooth Mountain. To the left of the rock is our first glimpse of Colorado's higher mountains with Longs Peak and the Indian Peaks Wilderness dominating the southern horizon.

Continuing the northern traverse, we'll navigate a couple more forks, staying on a westerly course at these junctions. Again, there are many social trails here and oftentimes the main trail alternates between long slabs of rock and dirt; remain prudent in following the designated path. Soon the trail leads down through a meadow right in front of the huge horse tooth and around to the north side where the hike up the rock is most accessible. A short scramble leads to a lofty perch, at 7255 feet, overlooking all of Fort Collins and Horsetooth Reservoir to the east. To the west, immediately below the rock, is a strangely graceful web of local access roads, and beyond are the high, snowy peaks of the back ranges. Due north is the landscape of Lory State Park, another excellent place to play.

Descend the rock the same way you came and follow the meadow trail, but at the first fork head right (southwest) on the loop section of this hike. This new route is a steady downhill that provides outstanding views to the west along a ridgeline. In short order the trail cuts left off the ridge and zigzags back down to an access road. The terrain will look familiar initially, as below and to the left is the creek, trail, and boulder line we followed coming up. The road gradually meanders down the south side of the mountain until it rejoins the Soderberg intersection. From here, it's an easy stroll back to the trailhead.

6 ELC LOOP

Round trip ■	**2.8 miles**
Loop direction ■	Counterclockwise
Hiking time ■	1 hour
Sweat factor ■	Low
Starting elevation ■	4880 feet
High point ■	4885 feet
Low point ■	4875 feet
Elevation gain ■	10 feet
Best hiking season ■	April through October
Maps ■	USGS Fort Collins; Colorado State University ELC map
Contact ■	Colorado State University College of Natural Resources

Driving directions: The Colorado State University Environmental Learning Center is located east of Fort Collins near the Cache la Poudre River. Follow Drake Road past Timberline Road for 1 mile. At a hard right-hand curve in the road, turn left onto the bumpy gravel road, cross the railroad tracks, and follow the road past the water treatment facility to a dead end. Parking is available on the right, along with information kiosks.

At the far eastern fringe of the bustling college town of Fort Collins, the Colorado State University Environmental Learning Center (ELC) offers more than 200 acres of forest, wetlands, a scenic river, and even resident raptors.

These lands are rich in history, dating to the 1800s. The Arapaho Indians hunted here and tribal councils were held on the center's grounds. Later, ELC land was the site of the Overland Trail stagecoach stop. The ELC began with 80 acres of land donated to the university in the 1960s, and CSU continues to manage the area through its College of Natural Resources. Hands-on environmental education is supported with a comprehensive education building and visitor center with an indoor classroom, outdoor amphitheater, and teaching forest. This place is a wonderful asset for the town and is ideal for wildlife viewing or taking a quiet stroll. This short hike explores some of the 2.5 miles of trails visiting several distinct ecosystems. The small building adjacent to the parking area houses the Rocky Mountain Raptor Program, a university-based resource dedicated to providing medical care, rehabilitation, and release for injured birds of prey. Walk over and take a gander at these striking avians—bald and golden eagles, great horned owls, hawks, and other birds native to the area.

The hike starts at the corner of the lot and follows the Poudre River Bike Trail for a short distance to a suspension bridge over Fossil Creek. On the other side we will hang a left at the fork in the trail, hiking along the creek

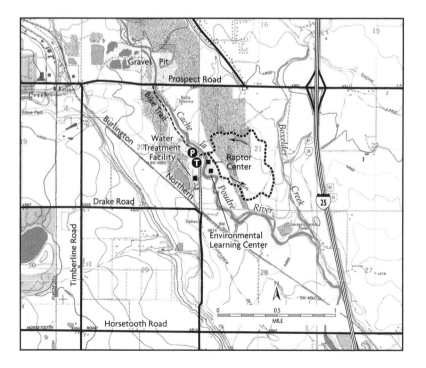

ELC trail

past huge cottonwoods. The path turns and heads almost due east toward the Poudre River, clearing the trees and entering a prairie landscape. Closer to the river we can hear the honks and quacks of ducks and geese on the water, along with more melodious tunes from various songbirds. The gentle current of the river flowing through the ELC belies its rugged origins far up in the high country. The Poudre begins as an alpine lake on the flanks of the Continental Divide, then tumbles through scenic forests and canyons to finally make its leisurely journey to the confluence with the South Platte River east of Greeley.

The trail turns south now, paralleling the river, rolling over a couple of hillocks and sagging through narrow gullies. Another fork arrives, with one option leading straight ahead and the other splitting off to the southwest, toward the woods. We'll head for the trees, passing one more field of prairie grasses along the way. The trail winds into a large stand of old-growth cottonwood, with nearly as many downed trees as there are standing trees. We've transitioned to a different ecosystem in just a few steps. This is top-shelf habitat for critters like white-tailed deer, elk, rabbits, and badger, and many species of birds. Stay alert and some of them are bound to show themselves. Our path winds past the aged trees and meets the suspension bridge at the creek once again. Head across and back to the trailhead to wrap up this short hike.

1 Devils Backbone Trail

Round trip ■	**4 miles**
Loop direction ■	Clockwise
Hiking time ■	3 hours
Sweat factor ■	Low+
Starting elevation ■	5102 feet
High point ■	5340 feet
Low point ■	5102 feet
Elevation gain ■	400 feet
Best hiking season ■	April through October
Maps ■	USGS Masonville; Larimer County Parks and Open Lands
Contact ■	Larimer County Parks and Open Lands

Driving directions: To get here, follow US 34 West from Loveland about 3 miles to Hidden Valley Drive, right before the big water tank. Turn right and follow the paved road to the trailhead on the left. Plenty of parking is available, but this is a popular trail and it can get crowded on weekends.

The unmistakable Devils Backbone on the outskirts of Loveland is a unique geologic treasure in Colorado. Impressive even from a distance, this row of vertical rocks is best seen up close to truly appreciate its rugged beauty. This path, a loop with tails on both ends, gets within spitting distance of the backbone and is a great trail for a quick hike or run. The Devils Backbone area includes more than 2100 acres of open land obtained with support from area cities and landowners. As with Boulder County and its Parks and Open Space program, Larimer County has also enjoyed success setting aside lands for recreation and heritage uses.

This is a multiuse path shared with horses and mountain bikers. Trail maps and brochures are stocked in the kiosk at the start.

Grab a map and let's head down the trail packed with red-orange soil and rock as it curves a couple of times to a northwesterly direction. The 1800s-era Louden Ditch intersects the southern end of the Open Space land and is still in use today to carry water from the Big Thompson River to farms and faucets to the east. A bridge crosses over a normally dry creekbed and continues on through a hillside of yucca, sage, and cactus. This area gets real hot from June all the way into autumn, so be prepared with enough water and sunscreen. A junction at approximately 0.8 mile splits the trail into foot travel only and both foot and bike travel. Let's choose the left,

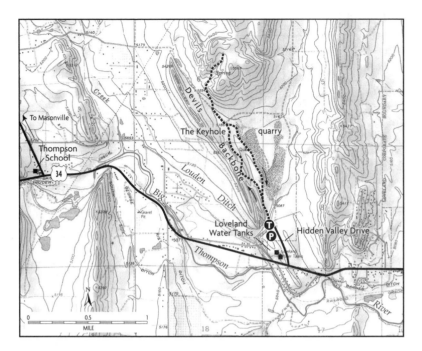

uphill route for hikers only and begin a moderate climb to an overlook and rest bench on a small plateau on the backbone itself. Don't climb on any of these rocks. More than 100 million years old, they are fragile and unstable. Stay on the trail and appreciate them from a distance.

This rock formation provides ideal nesting sites in its nooks and crannies for birds of several flavors. Red-tailed hawks, great horned owls, swallows, and a pair of ravens call this place home. The ravens, especially, are a treat, as it is rare to locate a nesting site. Posted signs at the start of the approach trail to these nesting areas list seasonal closure dates. Steer clear during those times and let the birds go about their nesting chores undisturbed.

The Keyhole, a distinctive window in one of the larger rocks of the spine, is a fun place to rest and take in great views of the mountains to the west and the plains to the east. From here, we have a short descent to the top part of the loop and a left turn onto the upper "tail" segment. We'll head along this path to the base of a huge hill, and start climbing along a dry drainage. Halfway up, we can catch our breath, turn around for super views, and go back toward the main loop. If you're in the mood for more, keep climbing up this hill; the trail joins two more loops for a longer, 7-mile hike. Back at the junction again, this time we take the low road and follow the eastern leg of the trail through low shrubbery and more yucca and cacti. Keep an eye out for rattlesnakes, bull snakes, and garter snakes. Don't worry too much about the rattlers—if you leave them alone, they won't bother you. This

Devils Backbone

lower trail follows the contour of the hill, meets the first junction, and then wanders back to the trailhead.

8 EAGLE WIND TRAIL

Round trip ■	**4 miles**
Loop direction ■	Clockwise
Hiking time ■	3.25 hours
Sweat factor ■	Low
Starting elevation ■	5496 feet
High point ■	5910 feet
Low point ■	5496 feet
Elevation gain ■	418 feet
Best hiking season ■	April through October
Maps ■	USGS Hygiene; Boulder County Parks and Open Space
Contact ■	Boulder County Parks and Open Space

Driving directions: The trailhead for this lollipop loop is at the end of North 53rd Street. Follow Colorado 66 west from Longmont, or east from

Lyons, to North 53rd and go north for 2 miles. The trail begins where the road ends. Restrooms and picnic tables are on site, as well as a kiosk containing interesting particulars about the area's history, flora, and fauna.

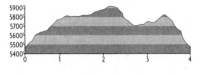

Boulder County's Parks and Open Space program has done a tremendous job of preserving area lands from the relentless crush of sprawl that is devouring the Front Range. Nearly 70,000 acres have been set aside to protect critical

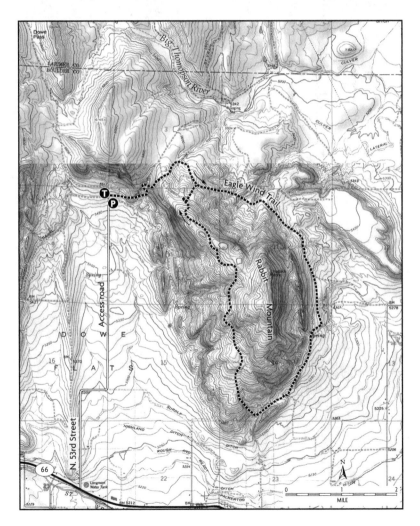

View of Indian Peaks and Longs Peak

wildlife habitat, ranches, and agricultural land, and to provide recreation opportunities for area residents and visitors. With the help of an extensive volunteer list, more than 80 miles of trails have been set aside for the enjoyment of multiple user groups. This is a short loop with fine views of Longs Peak to the west, the Indian Peaks and Flatirons to the south, and Loveland and the plains to the east. The multiuse trail (hikers, horses, mountain bikes) follows a ridge through grasslands and pine forests that are important habitat for wildlife like deer, hawks and eagles, and many species of songbirds. Rabbit Mountain, which this hike circumnavigates, is an ideal close-to-town destination and a popular choice for a quick getaway.

The dirt and gravel trail leads up the hillside east of the parking lot, making a couple of lazy switchbacks on its way to the top of the ridge. We mosey through a garden of yucca, sage shrubs, and cacti. Look for miner bees feeding on prickly pear cactus, a primary source of pollen for these busy insects. In short order the trail arrives at a junction and a sign for Eagle Wind Trail. A right turn here leads across a gravel road and the trail continues on the other side. Big views to the east open up here as the path climbs gradually to a fork in the trail. Let's be daring here and go left to start the loop. The tread is a mix of rocks and hard-packed dirt, and curves lazily through widely spaced ponderosa and big bluestem grass. Also in the mix is the mountain mahogany shrub, which is the final ingredient in a critical and diminishing plant association in Colorado. This mix of plants occurring where eastern grasslands meet forested foothills provides ideal habitat and forage for small mammals like mice and rabbits, and in turn for raptors like owls, eagles, and hawks. Look skyward for sightings of the big birds cruising the wind's currents. Look down to spot rattlesnakes, which are common in this area. Deer of both the white-tailed and mule variety also spend time on Rabbit Mountain, along with elusive mountain lions.

A gentle rise in elevation leads past a large open hillside and rounds the back side of the loop to begin its return, treating us to an impressive view of Longs Peak and a chunk of Mount Meeker straight to the west, and also another look at Boulder and the Flatirons in the distant south. Now the path heads into a stand of tall ponderosa, and for a short while we walk through a small forest. Chances are good in these trees, some as old as 300 years, to see woodpeckers, jays, flickers, and other species. Clearing the trees at their northern edge, we arrive at the fork and turn left back to the gravel road. Now it's simply a matter of following the trail back down the switchbacks to the trailhead and the end of this short hike.

9 RED ROCK LOOP

Round trip ■	**8 miles**
Loop direction ■	Clockwise
Hiking time ■	4.5 hours
Sweat factor ■	Moderate
Starting elevation ■	10,076 feet
High point ■	10,076 feet
Low point ■	9350 feet
Elevation gain ■	1477 feet
Best hiking season ■	Late June through October
Maps ■	USGS Ward
Contact ■	Roosevelt National Forest

Driving directions: The trailhead for this loop is located just off the Peak to Peak Scenic Byway (Colorado 72) right above the little mountain town of Ward. Follow Brainard Lake Drive, and ample signage, from the highway to the trailheads for the Sourdough and Red Rock Trails. Parking is available along the road and in a couple of renegade parking lots. Warning: the place fills up fast on weekends. Get here early.

This is a fun hike in the popular Brainard Lake Recreation Area west of Boulder. The trail descends steadily from the trailhead and crosses South St. Vrain Creek, then wanders through deep woods for its entire length, with only moderate climbs along the way. Pines give way to a grove of aspen as the path skirts by the edge of a secluded lake, and soon we hear the creek again as it tumbles down a waterfall into a small canyon. This area sees plenty of use, but most is concentrated close to Brainard Lake and the well-traveled Sourdough Trail south of the entrance road, leaving our trail peaceful and uncrowded.

The Sourdough trailhead is clearly marked heading south. Simply

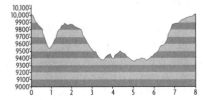

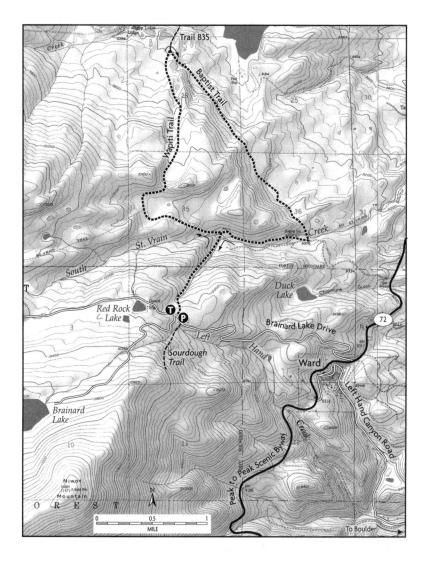

turn the other way and follow the gravel path to the signs for the Wapiti Trail. The initial sections of the trail are on gravel and rock, following a gradual descent past lodgepole and limber pine mixed with fir. Gigantic boulders lie partially concealed in the tall trees. Grays jays are a common sight through here, looking for a dropped handful of gorp or other treats. After 1 mile, we arrive at a wooden bridge crossing St. Vrain Creek. It's nice to linger at creek crossings to just look and listen, and this is one of the prettiest streams in all of Colorado. Lest we tarry too long, we'll press on, hiking on steadily rising ground to a junction and a sign announcing the Sourdough, Brainard Lake, and Wapiti Trails. The path to the right is the one we will follow on our return, so left we shall go, in the direction of Brainard Lake. The trail is littered with rocks as it climbs, curving gently closer to the creek on our left. Soon the grade levels and we enjoy a nice stroll on soft, almost bouncy tread through a park-like setting of huge trees with a clean understory, thick grasses, and boulders garnished with deep green moss.

Two miles brings us to the junction with Trail 835. We'll follow Baptist Trail to the right (southeast), climbing steeply on rocky ground into old lodgepole forest that has regenerated as a mix of spruce and fir after a long-ago fire. A few hundred steps later, the trail descends again, this time into a valley and a crossing of Beaver Creek. A relaxing walk through a pretty stand of aspen and an open meadow leads past the shoreline of a lake of unknown name. At 3 miles there is a fork, and we'll lean to the right, back again on rocky terrain in thicker woods. Another junction arrives in short order, and here we simply follow the sign leading the way to the Red Rock trailhead. There are some lazy rolling hills along this stretch for a little change of pace. Listen closely. Sounds like there might be a stream up ahead. Sure enough, the trail bends near the edge of a small gorge where South St. Vrain Creek tumbles in a mix of waterfalls and frothy rapids. This landmark means we are close to arriving at the junction with the sign for the Red Rock trailhead. At the junction we'll cross the bridge one more time and hoof it up the steady, mile-long ascent back to the trailhead.

10 ┆ BEAR PEAK LOOP

Round trip	■	6.2 miles
Loop direction	■	Counterclockwise
Hiking time	■	4.5 hours
Sweat factor	■	Moderate+
Starting elevation	■	6104 feet
High point	■	8461 feet
Low point	■	5970 feet
Elevation gain	■	2998 feet
Best hiking season	■	May through October
Maps	■	USGS Boulder; Boulder Mountain Parks
Contact	■	Boulder Mountain Parks

Driving directions: To reach the trailhead from south Boulder, follow Table Mesa Drive west from Colorado 93. The road ends at a huge parking lot for the National Center for Atmospheric Research; near the main entrance, a sign for the Mesa Trail leads the way.

Colorado's Front Range, extending nearly the entire distance between the state's borders north and south, offers a wonderful prelude to the rugged peaks of the higher mountains farther west. Arid slopes, hogback ridges, deep canyons, and areas of dense forest provide an ideal setting for great hiking, like this route in the hills near Boulder. Our hike begins in the midst of this striking range, at the southern reaches of Boulder and the National Center for Atmospheric Research (NCAR). Perched atop Table Mesa in the shadow of the Flatirons, NCAR is a renowned think tank researching complex happenings such as climate change, atmospheric composition, and weather formation and forecasting.

The route starts on the Walter Orr Roberts Interpretive Trail, following a wide, crushed gravel path through a stand of widely spaced ponderosa pine. The interpretive trail ends past the trees, merging into the Dakota Trail, which curves along an open slope to reveal great views of all of Boulder and the plains beyond. Boulder is the mother lode of throwback hippies, well-to-do college students, coffeehouses, elegant homes, and a lot of outdoor-lovin' folk. The Flatirons, the city's unmistakable landmark at its western border, rise abruptly from the foothills of the Front Range, providing a treasured and convenient mountain playground close to home. This miniature mountain range was born of nearly 300-million-year-old sedimentary rock that was lifted skyward by a major uplift of the Rockies, like the opening of a really heavy-duty drawbridge. The present day range is broken into individual, arrowhead-shaped sheets of smooth gray stone, with pointy peaks leaning sharply to the west.

Turning back to the south and into a second grove of ponderosa, our trail skirts the base of a stubby water tower. Look closely in this area for ripples embedded in the rock—135-million-year-old evidence that this land was once the coastline of an immense inland sea. The trail curves away from the trees, with a couple of rocky sections along the way, into wide, grassy hills and great views of the Flatirons. We arrive at the Mesa Trail at 1 mile. This is a well-maintained, major arterial trail running from Chautauqua Park all the way to Eldorado Springs. Take a left here and wind past another fork at the Mallory Cave Trail, a short path climbing up Dinosaur Mountain to the small cave. We'll continue south over roots and small rocks to a scenic glen beneath the high canyon walls of Bear Canyon. This is a great little spot to just stop and listen to the stream trickling alongside the trail, with rugged

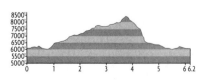

views westward up the canyon. Leaving the glen, the trail follows a couple of lazy curves to the Bear Canyon Trail cutoff. A sign for Bear Peak West Ridge points us in the right direction. Note the other sign

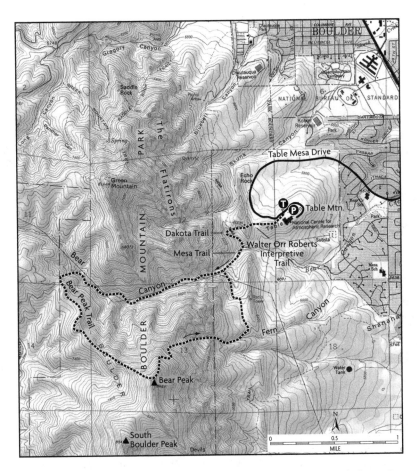

here that says "Recent Bear Activity In Area." Keep your eyes peeled; maybe our ursine luck will hold and we'll see one on the way.

Almost immediately we are treated to fantastic views of plains to the east as the trail winds uphill on a moderate grade past monstrous boulders and towering Douglas-fir. Small and medium-size rocks are scattered about the trail here, and higher up our path turns to stone as it travels right over some larger boulders in a tight section of the canyon. Farther along, we cross back and forth over Bear Creek a few times and into a scenic wetland area amid the rocky landscape, delving into thickets of scrub willow and copses of young aspen. Groundcover of mountain holly, wild rose, and juniper soften the rugged terrain. This is a splendid section of the trail and our favorite part of the hike, if not for the menacing powerline suspended over the canyon like an interminable dark cloud.

Take a look behind you for a glimpse at the summit of Bear Peak. It still

Early section of Bear Peak Trail

looks a long way off, and here the trail veers north, away from the peak, over a newly constructed bridge above the creek, before making a couple of switchbacks in a long arc around this basin. Then it moseys back southwest to the top of the ridge overlooking the creek below and superb views all around. The ski runs of Eldora and some higher summits in the Indian Peaks Wilderness are in sight in the not-too-distant west. Farther along the trail is a small meadow dabbled with ponderosa pine and at the other end we are treated to a fine view of the rugged crown of Longs Peak to the north.

At the approach of 4 miles, a long view opens of the canyon below, and we begin the final ascent of Bear Peak over loose rocks and a steeper grade. After passing a large scree slope, we'll need to clamber over giant boulders and grunt up steep and tight switchbacks to reach the summit. Sweeping 360-degree views reward our uphill efforts. The High Plains open up far to the east, and the other three directions unveil Denver's skyline (on non-smoggy days) and mountains in various shapes and sizes, including Mount Audubon to the west and Rocky Mountain National Park's treasured peaks to the north.

After a short break, it's time to head down. We'll follow the sign for Fern

Canyon, which sounds like a tranquil enough place, right? Before we reach the canyon proper, however, the trail follows a loose, and steep, talus field filled with big, angular rocks that threaten to bend ankles in unfavorable directions. Use caution here and stay light on your feet. Back in the woods, we pass a mammoth boulder of unimaginable heft painted with squiggly striations of flushed rose and chestnut. The woods are shaded and lush with green foliage, the trail soft with a carpet of pine needles, and more beefy boulders are scattered about among the trees. At the 5-mile mark, we pass a sign announcing falcon breeding grounds in the area to our left. February through July are the busy months for the birds, so give them some privacy and steer clear this time of the year.

The canyon becomes narrow and steeper as it descends, following several stairstep routes over small rocks along the way. At just over 6 miles, we'll follow the sign for Bear Creek and Shanahan Trails, enjoying an easier grade back into ponderosa pine and a drier landscape. At the junction with the Mesa Trail, a right turn leads to Eldorado Springs and beyond; we'll go left and follow our earlier route back to the trailhead and the conclusion of the loop.

11 ┆ MOUNT SANITAS

Round trip ■	**3.4 miles**
Loop direction ■	Clockwise
Hiking time ■	2+ hours
Sweat factor ■	Moderate
Starting elevation ■	5520 feet
High point ■	6863 feet
Low point ■	5520 feet
Elevation gain ■	1343 feet
Best hiking season ■	April through October
Maps ■	USGS Boulder; Boulder County Parks; Boulder Mountain Parks
Contact ■	Boulder County Parks and Open Space; Boulder Mountain Parks

Driving directions: The hike begins at the base of Sunshine Canyon, at the west end of Mapleton Avenue in Boulder. To reach the trailhead, follow Mapleton Avenue west from Broadway 0.8 mile to the trailhead. Two small parking areas along the road provide access to the trail.

Here is a short trip on a popular path at the base of Sunshine Canyon, toward the north end of Boulder. The loop follows rocky tread through sparse ponderosa

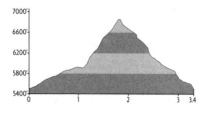

to the summit of Mount Sanitas, and descends an open hillside to return on a wide gravel path. With easy access and proximity to town, this trail is a favorite of hikers, runners, and climbers. It is common to see super-fit people running on this trail, and halfway up the initial ascent is a collection of huge boulders, cliffs, and rock formations that attract technical climbers. True to form with many Front Range hikes, Sanitas offers superb views of Boulder and the eastern plains. The climb to the summit is steady but not grueling, and the descent is mellow and finishes with an easy stroll to the trailhead.

This hike starts as a wide, rocky path and points uphill right from the gun. We'll start by climbing a stairstep route through stands of ponderosa, as fine views of the western mountains emerge with the steady increase in altitude. A few social trails branch off the main path to overlooks along the way, including several trails leading to dedicated bouldering and climbing

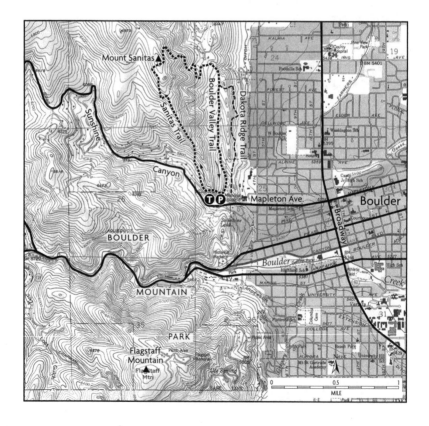

areas. (No hiking is allowed in these areas. Observe climbers from a distance.) Many of the big slabs of rock are branded with chalky handprints or are otherwise dusted in a fine film of white.

The grade lessens a bit once past the climbing areas, at times even leveling off, as the trail passes through dispersed ponderosa to a small clearing. A gathering of gray-brown boulders adorned in soft lichens surround a smattering of grasses and low shrubbery. Continuing higher, we alternately hike through stands of pine and open sections of grasses to roughly 1.3 miles and a final scramble up the jumble of huge rocks that make up the summit of Mount Sanitas. Take a short break and ogle the stunning views to the east, then begin the sketchy descent down a steep, rocky stairstep route. Back into another ponderosa stand, our path takes us right through the side of a colossal boulder, around and over numerous rocks of all sizes, then past another shaped like a giant duckbill. The trail is faint at times in this area, but reassuring

Up toward Mount Sanitas

hiking signs help lead the way. As the path clears the trees, we pass through talus slopes littered with thick, flat rocks jutting chaotically from the hillside, and spiny yucca plants and other stubby foliage.

At this point, we also come upon a sign for the vanished Sanitas Quarries, which were burrowed into this hillside in the 1920s. Portions of this section of the trail were once wagon roads providing access to the quarries. The quarries were significant in Boulder's history, providing material for many buildings in the area. *Sanitas* is Latin for "sanitarium," and Mount Sanitas is named after the Colorado Sanitarium formerly located at the base of this hill. In 1969, the Boulder County Parks and Open Space program bought the quarries and surrounding land, and now the area is protected from any future disturbance and is used for recreation and wildlife habitat.

Our trail continues to descend on red, sandy soil through a plantation of yucca plants and other stubby foliage, with nary a tree in sight. Near the base of the hill, the yucca gives way to grasses as we turn south to the final stretch, a gentle descent on the wide gravel of the Boulder Valley Trail. The Dakota Ridge Trail wanders the woods to the east, offering more of a squiggly path back to the trailhead. The Boulder Valley Trail makes a beeline toward Mapleton Avenue, crossing a riparian area and creek bed near the end, and coasts back to the trailhead.

12 ┆ BOULDER VALLEY RANCH

Round trip ■	**3.2 miles**
Loop direction ■	Counterclockwise
Hiking time ■	1.5 to 2 hours
Sweat factor ■	Low
Starting elevation ■	5336 feet
High point ■	5525 feet
Low point ■	5296 feet
Elevation gain ■	320 feet
Best hiking season ■	Year-round
Maps ■	USGS Boulder
Contact ■	Boulder County Parks and Open Space

Driving directions: From the intersection of Broadway (Colorado 7) and US 36, drive north on US 36 for 1 mile out of Boulder. Take a right onto Longhorn Road and drive another 1.1 miles to the Boulder Valley Ranch parking area.

This gentle and fun loop is located in the Boulder Valley Ranch open space north of town. Extremely popular among Boulder's fittest, these trails are packed with runners, bikers, and horseback riders. This trail is perfect for a great trail run or an excuse to take lunch outdoors. Four different trails take us through prairie dog colonies, past a natural wetland, and offer some of the best views of Boulder in the area. The counterclockwise direction of the hike makes for a manageable ascent and a leisurely cruise on the return. It can get crowded here, though, so come out early.

From the parking area, the trail strikes out west on the Cobalt Trail, following a long plateau on the left through an arid setting of yucca, cacti, and

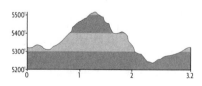

shrubs. Directly west are the northern foothills of Boulder, softly rolling out of sight to the north toward Lyons. We will pass through the first of a few gates that section off livestock in the area. Make sure to close all gates

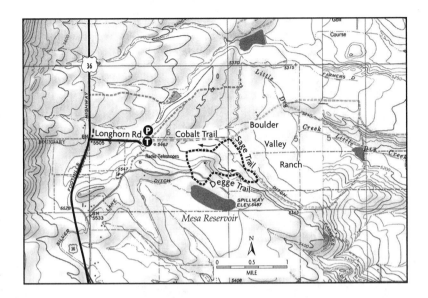

behind you to dissuade an errant cow or two from wandering off. Stop often and listen; there are a variety of songbirds singing happily, and assorted chirps and squeaks confirm we are in the vicinity of prairie dogs. We will pass a few different colonies on this short trek, and our intrusion will not go unannounced, as sentries will sound our arrival to these interesting and controversial societies. In fact, prairie dogs have eleven distinctive chirps for different kinds of communication. The City of Boulder Open Space and Mountain Parks department has played an active role in helping protect these animals from poisoning and target practice, and allows us to enjoy them today.

As we get closer to 1 mile in, the trail becomes wider and rockier as it climbs gently toward the first junction. At around 0.9 mile, there is an access road that we will cross via two gates, and on the other side follow the sign indicating the Hidden Valley Trail, which drops down into a large meadow filled with hundreds more of our squeaky friends. Heading south now on a narrow dirt trail, we get our first glimpses of Boulder's Flatirons off in the distance. The trail crosses a small culvert and parallels a gulch, and just a bit farther ahead, we will turn left and go east on the Degge Trail, dropping even lower into this small valley. Continuing straight and east past another junction and gate, new sounds come into earshot. A large riparian habitat encompasses a significant portion of this open space, with croaking frogs, mallards, and geese often serenading the area with melodic tunes; a beautiful and seemingly out-of-place variety of water-loving plants also spring forth in this area. Cottonwoods, willows, and cattails are just a few among the many riparian plants that make an interesting scene when juxtaposed with the nearby cacti and junipers.

The "hardest" climb of the day comes alongside the wetlands as the trail snakes its way to the top of this plateau. From here, we get a wonderful 360-degree view of our surroundings. Green and Bear Mountains flank the Flatirons down south; Mount Sanitas is a little farther north. Boulder Reservoir and Haystack Mountain lie to the east and northeast. The trail meets up with a much larger path and becomes a multiuse trail from here on out. We'll continue east toward another split in the trail, then turn left, passing through a gate onto the Sage Trail. Great views of the reservoir, Boulder Valley Ranch, and our return path, lined with cottonwoods, come into view down below. From the top of this plateau, the trail steeply descends to the last junction. This is a favorite hill for mountain bikers to bomb down or grit their teeth to practice climbing. Be aware of your surroundings around here, and be sure to yield right of way when appropriate.

At the bottom, we will make a hard left turn back northwest to finish this short loop. The path is wide and parallels a ditch giving life to a number of trees and plants. From here, it's just a short jaunt back to the beginning of this great local gem.

Hiking the Boulder Valley Ranch trails

13 | BURRO LOOP

Round trip ■	**5.4 miles**
Loop direction ■	Counterclockwise
Hiking time ■	2 to 3 hours
Sweat factor ■	Moderate
Starting elevation ■	7872 feet
High point ■	9064 feet
Low point ■	7872 feet
Elevation gain ■	1920 feet
Best hiking season ■	May through October
Maps ■	USGS Black Hawk
Contact ■	Colorado State Parks, Golden Gate Canyon

Driving directions: To get there, drive north from Golden on Colorado 93 for 1 mile. Turn left onto Golden Gate Canyon Road and drive for 13 miles to the entrance to Golden Gate Canyon State Park. The park requires a $5 entry fee, then proceed northeast to the Bridge Creek parking area.

In the 1840s, settlers moved into the present-day site of Golden Gate Canyon State Park in search of gold, but it was some 6 miles southwest in Blackhawk and Central City where the gold was to be found. The Golden Gate Toll Road was constructed to bypass this beautiful area in order to reach the prosperous towns. While no gold has ever been found within the park, there are plenty of other treasures hidden here, and the Burro Loop is no exception. This hike offers a variety of landscapes to hikers and scenery ranging from sheltered riparian corridors to the entirety of the eastern plains or massive snowcapped mountains.

From the Bridge Creek parking area, we begin our lollipop hike by hooking west and then north up the Burro Trail. No worries about getting lost on this trail; just follow the signs with the burro hoofprint. The path crests a little knoll and works its way east on wide, rocky tread amidst a landscape of ponderosa and aspen to a junction with the Mountain Lion Trail. Veer left here and continue up the Burro Trail toward Windy Peak. Heading northeast and descending before climbing, the trail deteriorates a bit, with root tentacles that cling to passing boots, scattered rocks, and often greasy, slippery mud. The descent takes us through a dense coniferous area, but when the trail bottoms out next to a lazy stream, there is a notable

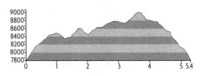

transition from the typical aridity of Colorado to a riparian humidor akin to the lands of the Oregon coast. Lush grasses, willows, and wild raspberry plants create a wonderfully verdant corridor of heavy air. The trail parallels the creek for a stretch and crosses a small wooden bridge before resuming its gain in elevation. Just past 1 mile, we'll reach a junction marking the beginning of the loop portion of the hike. Let's continue east, following the Burro Trail along the creek for a counterclockwise loop.

The trail becomes overgrown with grasses and branches tickling your legs, but in just a few dozen steps, it wraps north away from the creek and widens significantly. Can you feel the difference in the air? Indeed, we've hiked "back" into Colorado, passing through a wide meadow with dry, tall grasses, scattered wildflowers and a smattering of ponderosa pine. We'll pass a few service roads on this wide, gravelly trail before turning left toward Windy Peak at

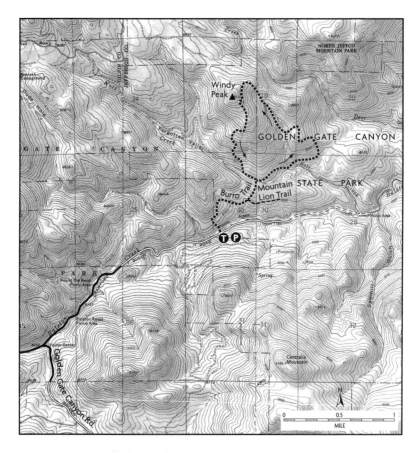

Opposite: Golden flowers along the Burro Loop

about 1.5 miles. As we begin the first significant elevation gain of the day, this east-facing hillside exposes the mountains to the east across the valley, the last defense between the park and the wide-open plains beyond. The tread turns to loose rocks and the slope gets rather steep as the trail curls west. After a few switchbacks, our legs earn a brief reprieve on a little knoll and soon we enter a thicker stand of ponderosa and fir, which brings us to 2.5 miles and the high point in the loop. If you feel energetic, it's only about a half-mile to the summit of Windy Peak and some fine views all around.

It's all down hill from here, following the sign for the Burro Trail toward the Bridge Creek parking area. The trail undulates gently at first as it turns south, then begins to descend rapidly, moving through this thickly wooded area before popping out of the trees to reveal more views to the east. There is a wonderful bird's eye perspective of the topography of the area from here—with the eastern plains for comparison, it is truly humbling to see how the small creeks in the area slowly cut through mountainsides creating the valleys, meadows, and gorges all around. The trail also slithers past large rock formations that seem to materialize from the side of the mountain, and for a brief moment, views far to the south are exposed, including the monster peaks of the Front Range: Pikes, Evans, Grays, and Torreys. As we hike lower and lower, the grade of the mountain becomes more moderate and begins to turn back east. A short jaunt north leads to one more junction and the completion of the actual loop; a right turn takes us back down to the Bridge Creek area.

14 WALKER RANCH

Round trip ■	**7.6 miles**
Loop direction ■	Counterclockwise
Hiking time ■	3 hours
Sweat factor ■	Moderate
Starting elevation ■	7200 feet
High point ■	7411 feet
Low point ■	6360 feet
Elevation gain ■	1931 feet
Best hiking season ■	March through November
Maps ■	USGS Boulder
Contact ■	Roosevelt National Forest

Driving directions: Simply driving to this hike's trailhead is a pleasure as the route follows steep and curvy Flagstaff Road above Boulder for some impressive city views. From US 36, turn west onto Baseline Road. Follow Baseline past Chautauqua Park and up Flagstaff Road. There are two parking areas 8 miles past the base of the mountain on the left side of the road. The first serves as spillover and winter parking; the second (about 0.25 mile past) is right at the trailhead.

This popular multiuse trail travels over moderate elevation change and through wide, open valleys and dense woods, and moseys along a rushing creek. It's a wonderfully maintained trail, perfect for all abilities. The area is offset far enough from Boulder to feel isolated, but its proximity makes it a favorite among the city's flourishing outdoor community.

From the trailhead, we are immediately led southwest on the wide South Boulder Creek Trail. The trail makes one long switchback past an abrupt column of rock formations as it heads south through sweeping grasses, yucca, and cacti. Spacious views, in large part due to the 1000-acre Eldorado Fire in 2000, expose an eastern glance to the backs of Boulder's signature Flatirons and the rolling green hills of ponderosa pine that lead west. The path descends quickly past an array of informational signs concerning the flora and fauna of the area, as well as a detailed explanation of the fire that created the scraggly reminders of a once resplendent forest.

Heading farther down and out of the burn, the trail enters a dense stand of ponderosa and Douglas-fir. We'll cross a small gulch and at 1 mile we meet the rush of South Boulder Creek and a peaceful picnic area. From here, the wide, flat trail gently ascends west along the boulder-strewn creek. At 1.4 miles, we cross over a wooden bridge and immediately turn left at a junction, following the signs for the Walker Ranch Loop. After a steep switch to the east, we continue south away from the creek. Take a look over your shoulder and check out the contrast between the fire-scarred, south-facing slope and the lush green hill we're climbing now. The noisy rush of the creek soon disappears and around mile 2 we trek into the western reaches of Eldorado Canyon State Park. The trail flattens a little and reveals more sweeping views from east to west before plunging back into a forest of ponderosa, Douglas-fir, and juniper. Keep following signs for the loop hike at 2.2 miles, up a few switchbacks toward the Crescent Meadows parking lot.

The trail levels as it meets the parking lot, and out to the west the tips of the Indian Peaks jut above the horizon. At 2.6 miles, we'll turn left and begin heading east on the Crescent Meadows Trail. The narrow dirt trail slices down though an open, exposed valley of meadow grasses. The sun is relentless here, and the valley feels like a huge sauna until we begin to wrap northeast. Even with the assistance of some widely scattered ponderosas, there is little relief from the elements. But our sweat-blurred vision still sees beautiful views through Eldorado Canyon and out to southern Boulder and beyond to the east. Switchbacks hither and yon guide us gently down this valley, exposing the best views of the back of the Front Range all the while.

A surprise awaits just past 4.5 miles. Signs indicate a biker dismount

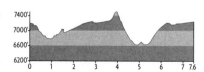

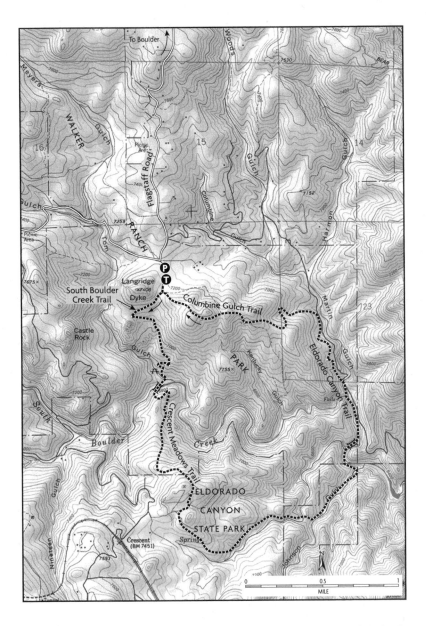

zone and horses are altogether not allowed as the trail begins a steep hike back down to the creek. Wooden risers stairstep down into this narrow canyon with the roiling creek below. From here, we walk by a series of pools in the creek, each spilling into the next. Large cutthroat, rainbow, and brown trout can be

Steep section of the Walker Ranch trail

seen patiently waiting for a variety of insects to come splashing into range. There are a number of comfortably smooth rocks nearby for elevated viewing of the fishy entertainment. Immediately after leaving the creek, we cross another large bridge and continue heading straight and north past the junction with the Eldorado Canyon Trail. From here, we'll be ascending nearly all of the remainder of the trip as this wide path follows a roller coaster of long stretches of climbing, and short transitional descents.

At 5.9 miles, we step onto the Columbine Gulch Trail and turn left toward the South Boulder Creek parking area. As the trail crosses over several feeder drainages, trees close in around us in corridors of shade and wildflowers decorate the path's borders. Just past a small footbridge, the trail gets steeper as it continues west, switchbacking up and out of a dense stand of pines to the final high point of the day. Take a last glimpse out to Boulder and cruise along a few more rolls in the mountainside back to the trailhead.

15 CANYON LOOP

Round trip ■	3.2 miles
Loop direction ■	Clockwise
Hiking time ■	1.5 hours
Sweat factor ■	Low+
Starting elevation ■	6548 feet
High point ■	6564 feet
Low point ■	6193 feet
Elevation gain ■	380 feet
Best hiking season ■	Year-round
Maps ■	USGS Boulder
Contact ■	Roosevelt National Forest

Driving directions: To reach the western trailhead from US 36 in Boulder, turn west onto Canyon Boulevard or Colorado 119 and drive 6.5 miles into the foothills. Turn right and drive north on Sugarloaf Road for 1 mile, then take a right onto Betasso Road. Drive 0.5 mile to the western trailhead on the left.

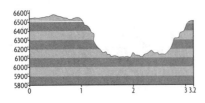

This short hike is close to Boulder, but tucked far enough west to offer seclusion. Located in the Betasso Preserve, home to a wide variety of plant and animal life and age-old geological formations, this 3.2-mile loop is maintained by Boulder County Parks and Open Space, which ensures a well-maintained and easily accessible trail all year long. From dense trees and gullies to open meadows and sweeping vistas, this rolling landscape offers the beautiful views and mellow climate that is so characteristic of the foothills of the Rocky Mountains.

At the western trailhead is a nice, sheltered picnic facility with restrooms and a kiosk providing maps and information about the area. From the kiosk,

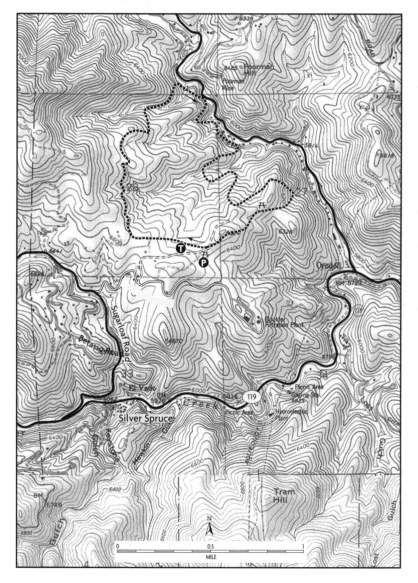

let's strike out northwest for a clockwise loop. This well-preserved area boasts a wide, multiuse trail with strict rules in effect to alleviate conflicts between user groups. Remain conscious and considerate and remember the trail was designed for us all. We begin through an open valley with tall grasses such as blue gamma and cheatgrass, yucca plants, and scattered ponderosas. Nearby rolling mountains straggle westward to the barely visible Indian Peaks and, if you look carefully, canyon openings provide glimpses out to the eastern plains. The trail makes a couple of bends to the west while heading north and soon leads into a grove of extra-large ponderosas and past one of a few strategically placed benches along the hike for enjoying the aesthetics of Boulder Canyon and neighboring foothills.

Before long we descend a northeast-facing slope into a more heavily wooded area. As with most Boulder County parks, the trail is both well maintained and well designed as it eases down the mountain by way of

Descending into ponderosa pines in Betasso Preserve

the contours in the hillside. In and out of small gulches we go until at about 0.7 mile we reach a small bluff affording more views of this ancient area. Geologists have dated the rock that lies beneath our feet as far back as 1.7 billion years. The path continues to descend, rolling in and out of the contours of the mountain and through small drainages into dense woods of ponderosa, juniper, and Douglas-fir. Just past 1 mile, the trail jumps out above a gully down to the left and leans into a north-facing bend. This part of the trail gets icy during the winter and can be muddy after a good rain; use caution accordingly. At 1.8 miles, the path traverses the main drainage of the area and we've reached the low point in the hike. From the creek, we ascend south and west, where the trail latches onto yet another ravine in this topographically diverse area, rambling past stands of fir trees on this cooler, wetter, north-facing side. At close to 2.4 miles, the change in environment becomes palpable as we crest a small bluff into the sunshine; the overlook hosts another bench perfect for a quick break and great views out east. From this point, the trail wanders west back in the direction of the trailhead. The path widens and the grade eases as it enters another large stand of healthy ponderosa, and more of the primordial rocks of the area poke out in various outcroppings amidst the trees. At 2.7 miles, the trail saunters past a junction with the eastern trailhead that also features some picnic tables and more nice spots to extend the trip with a picnic. To finish the loop, keep following the signs for the Canyon Loop Trail by continuing west up this wide, flat trail back to the trailhead.

16 DEVILS THUMB

Round trip ■	**14.7 miles**
Loop direction ■	Clockwise
Hiking time ■	12 hours
Sweat factor ■	High+
Starting elevation ■	9051 feet
High point ■	12,300 feet
Low point ■	9051 feet
Elevation gain ■	3394 feet
Best hiking season ■	May through September
Maps ■	USGS Monarch Lake
Contact ■	Roosevelt National Forest, Indian Peaks Wilderness

Driving directions: To reach the Hessie trailhead, head west from Nederland on County Road 130 and continue past the exit to Eldora Ski Area. About a half-mile after the paved road turns to dirt, there are signs and parking for the Hessie trailhead. Four-wheel-drive vehicles can turn left toward the signs and drive up a rugged path to the actual trailhead.

The Indian Peaks Wilderness Area northwest of Denver is one of the most popular in the state, and this loop is a big reason why. Hikers can look forward to two long, verdant valleys, a couple of outrageously beautiful

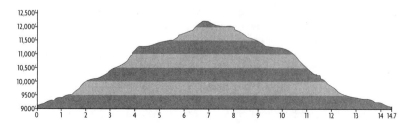

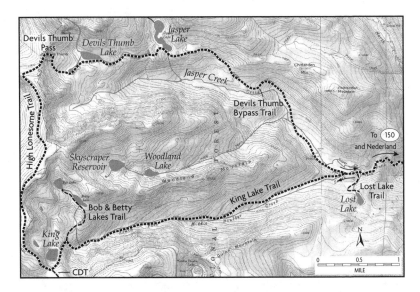

mountain passes, a stretch along the Continental Divide Trail with all-over views, and three lakes strung out along the hike like pearls, each offering a number of great campsites. Add in some plump hillsides glowing with colorful wildflowers and this wilderness is a beauty indeed, but it is also heavily used due to proximity to swelling population centers along the Front Range. Camping requires permits, and a late start, especially on weekends, will guarantee some additional mileage just hiking to the trailhead from a distant parking place. So choose a beautiful weekday, get here early, and discover why this area is such a Colorado gem.

The journey begins by heading west across a large wooden bridge onto a wide, rocky trail that immediately makes one large switchback up to the north through a scenic mix of aspen and pine. To our left, long, spidery, treeless paths mark the western edge of Eldora, a small ski area that is a favorite with locals. The width and tread of the beginning of this trail is just shy of being a paved road and is absolutely necessary given the heavy use of this extremely popular area. Before long, the rushing sounds of the upper reaches of Boulder Creek come into earshot and at 0.85 mile, we'll turn left toward the King Lake Trail by crossing the creek on another large wooden bridge. The trail gains elevation as it hugs the chattering creek, which crashes and spills over fallen logs and an array of large boulders. About 1 mile into the hike, we'll mosey away from the creek into a pleasant and lush undergrowth of willow and fir, following a collection of partially buried wooden risers as the trail ascends toward the junction with the Lost Lake Trail. Keep heading straight and to the west toward King Lake as a tree-lined basin opens up on our right, with the confluence of Jasper and Boulder Creeks far below. After a couple more wooden bridges, we reach our last early junction in the hike at 1.2 miles. Let's turn left on the King Lake Trail and aim for the long valley toward King Lake and the Continental Divide. Just shy of 1.5 miles, the trail wanders into the Indian Peaks Wilderness. This beautiful 75,000-acre area, named for a number of Native American tribes that resided here, is barely holding up to the constant assault of visitors year after year. As a result, there are many restrictions and regulations to ensure the area's preservation for future generations. Please pay close attention to all posted signs and be sure to procure the proper permits and instructions for camping from local ranger stations. Most of all, use your noggin out here and stay on designated trails, pack out trash, and go easy on the land.

That said, our path begins a long, slow ascent up the valley floor cradling Boulder Creek, dropping a wee bit south as it leads to the west. Slowly but surely, this valley's walls rise from the landscape to the north and south. Stands of pine open and close around us, offering glimpses every now and again of towering, serrated rocks. At this point, the majority of other hikers are left behind, but a sight high on our left still hints of civilization, albeit a very nostalgic sort. The antiquated Boulder Wagon Road curves out of the landscape on precarious wooden supports a thousand feet above our heads. The valley becomes noticeably tighter as it approaches the Divide, and the trail gets steeper near tree line, exposing more and more sweeping views of this massive hallway of high rock walls. At 4.5 miles, the switchbacks begin, zigzagging north and affording tremendous views of one side of this large glacial basin. The hiking is tough, but the emergence of handsome wildflowers and further exposure of the Continental Divide are welcome distractions. When the switchbacks end, the trail straightens out a little to the west again, and passes the junction for the Bob and Betty Lakes Trail. The landscape has become terraced with knolls and rock outcroppings, subalpine fir, short grasses, and wildflowers, all set in a mammoth cirque basin. Yelping marmots announce our arrival to King Lake at 5.2 miles. The elegant lake sits at about 11,400 feet and is bordered by a steep cliff on the west side, the top of which is the mighty Continental Divide. A small hillock on the other side of the lake offers a great place to relax and soak in the views of the curving ridgeline to the north, which is our next destination.

The trail wanders along the eastern side of the lake and begins climbing toward the Divide. This is the first of two steep climbs, with increasingly impressive views to the north. At 5.4 miles, we'll reach the epic Continental Divide Trail (CDT) on a saddle between Rollins Pass to the southeast and an even steeper ascent to the northwest. Check out the beautiful views of the mountains to the south as well as the skinny fingers of Winter Park Ski area. Let's turn right toward the Devils Thumb Trail and begin the second part of the climb toward the high point in the hike. The squiggly dirt trail does little to ease the climb, instead shooting straight into the heights of the alpine tundra. But somehow the steep steps seem effortless because we are climbing into our beloved high country—open hills swaddled in soft green

Devils Thumb Pass

mosses speckled with miniature flowers of pink, purple, yellow, and red, and slender rivulets hidden among spongy bulges of turf trickling down the Divide. Magical views in all directions leave us as breathless as the high altitude. This is what high-country hiking's all about.

From here, there is a strange split in the trail where the High Lonesome Trail hugs the top of the Divide while the CDT parallels it a few hundred yards below and to the west. Both trails lead north to the next junction, but we recommend remaining on the High Lonesome Trail as it is easier to find the turnoff. The trail follows the ridge and offers unrestricted views of the Indian Peaks leading off into Rocky Mountain National Park to the north. Approaching 8 miles, the trail enters the saddle south of Devils Thumb Pass. Follow the cairns carefully as they lead toward the northern edge of this saddle and the start of a long descent. At 8.2 miles, the trail makes a sharp right turn off the ridge toward Devils Thumb Lake. The grade here is treacherous, especially when lugging a big pack, as the path winds down loose rocks and gravel toward a lake tucked in a large basin. The magnificence of the area makes gawking irresistible, so stop first to sightsee lest you take a header. The terrain at the bottom is flatter and includes the first of two beautiful lakes nestled below steep walls of rock. As the trail continues to wander east toward Devils Thumb Lake, we get a better angle of the jutting namesake rock for this area up to the northwest. Shortly after 9 miles, we will pass over the outlet of Devils Thumb Lake and plunge back into tree line.

Soon the trail moseys into lands similar to the long valley ascent along Boulder Creek. Wildflowers and dense stands of pine create an attractive setting as we descend at a mellow and manageable rate. At 10 miles, the trail cruises past Jasper Lake, another great area for camping. A half-mile past the footbridge that crosses the outlet of Jasper Lake, continue east past the junction with the Diamond Lake Trail. From here, we begin a long, erratic descent over a wide and rocky track. The trail can be muddy at times as a number of drainages pass this way en route to Jasper Creek. Jasper's rumble becomes louder and louder before the noisy creek makes its appearance on our right-hand side. At 12.3 miles, we'll come to the junction with the Devils Thumb Bypass Trail, where we'll turn left and take the bypass downhill, darting in and out of trees before entering a gorgeous, wide open valley. Take in your last views of the glorious Divide as we leave the wilderness area at the far end of the valley. From here, the trail explores one last lush forest of spruce and fir and tags along again with the tumbling Jasper Creek. A final switchback leads down to the first junction and the short trip back to the trailhead to close a fantastic hike.

17 ■ BARR LAKE STATE PARK

Round trip ■	**8.8 miles**
Loop direction ■	Clockwise
Hiking time ■	3.5 hours
Sweat factor ■	Low+
Starting elevation ■	5100 feet
High point ■	5151 feet
Low point ■	5038 feet
Elevation gain ■	113 feet
Best hiking season ■	Year-round
Maps ■	USGS Brighton
Contact ■	Colorado State Parks, Barr Lake

Driving directions: To get here, take Interstate 76 north from Denver and turn east onto Bromley Lane. Drive east to Piccadilly Road, turn south and look for signs for the park entrance. As with all Colorado state parks, a daily pass is required to enjoy the park and may be purchased at the park entrance or the nature center.

Relating his views of honking geese at his Wisconsin farm, Aldo Leopold said, " . . . and in this annual barter of food for light, and winter warmth for summer solitude, the whole continent receives a net profit of a wild poem dropped from the murky skies upon the muds of March." At Barr Lake State Park, this wild poem is heard throughout winter, and there is much, much more. Geese, eagles, hawks, owls, and cormorants make up five of the 350 species of birds that have been spotted within this park. A bird-watcher's paradise, this hike takes an 8.8-mile journey around the lake, through a wildlife refuge, across an elevated dam with endless views, and provides shelters for bird-watching and picnic areas, too.

Starting on the east side of the lake, our hike takes off from the nature center parking area. Be sure to stop in to check out displays, grab a copy of the *Oasis Newsletter*, and speak to the friendly staff concerning any bird-related questions and information on guided bird walks and other public programming, or just to borrow some binoculars. From the parking area, we cross over a large wooden bridge and turn left to hike a clockwise loop, wandering immediately into the Barr Lake Wildlife Refuge, which occupies the southern half of the lake. Boating, fishing, pets, and fires are all prohibited on this southern half of the lake. We begin by heading south along a wide, flat road between the lake and the Denver and Hudson Canal. The big, beautiful cottonwoods lining the lake's shores are set against sweeping vistas that cover the Front Range as far south and north as the eye can see, from Mount Evans to the Indian Peaks, Longs Peak, and other high mountains to the north. Although this main trail is set away from the immediate shoreline of the lake, a couple of other paths stem off to provide direct access. Throughout the course of the hike, these subsidiary trails lead to boardwalks, picnic areas, and viewing benches. The trail winds its way west and wraps along the lake's southern reaches, and at 0.75 mile we'll pass one of the three wildlife observation stations. From here, the trail passes a junction with the Fox Meadow Trail, another side trail providing more immediate access to the shore, and we will reach one of a few small viewing pipes at 1.3 miles. Take a peek through the cylinder at the enormous nests of the bald eagles that call Barr Lake home. Shortly past this viewing spot is the access to the gazebo boardwalk. It is certainly worth the short walk that leads out over the lake to the small gazebo, equipped with a spotting scope for close-up bird-watching.

At 2.3 miles, the trail turns right off the main route and passes over a wooden bridge at the southernmost tip of the lake before reuniting with

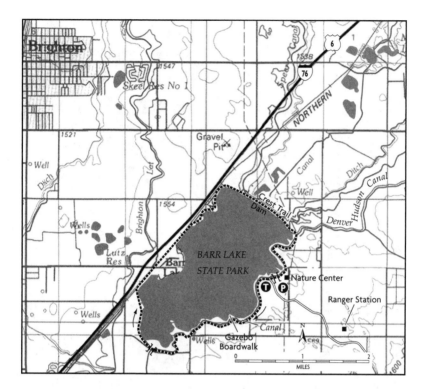

the wider path and ambling up to the western side of the lake. Nearing mile 3, the trail parallels Interstate 76, which adds the unwelcome drone of traffic to the solitude of the park, and then winds east away from the interstate to Barr Lake Village. At 4.5 miles, the trail leaves the wildlife refuge and heads for the northern shore of the lake and its accompanying dam. Be sure to follow the signs as the trail flirts with private property through this section.

Known as the Crest Trail, the road across the dam is open to hikers and bikers but not horses. It also should be noted that it is closed to everyone on Wednesdays and Saturdays during waterfowl hunting season (October to February). The trail below the dam accommodates hikers during these closures. Timing this hike to reach the Crest Trail at sunset is highly recommended. The western sky will stage a brilliant light show during long summer Colorado evenings; to the southeast, Denver International Airport's pointy white roof makes an attempt to imitate the mountains. At 7.3 miles, the dam ends and the hike turns south, making its way back to the nature center. After one more boardwalk and wildlife station, and the area's three picnic areas, the trail arrives back at the trailhead.

Sunset over Barr Lake

18 | WHITE RANCH PARK

Round trip ■ **4.8 miles**
Loop direction ■ Clockwise
Hiking time ■ 2 to 3 hours
Sweat factor ■ Low+
Starting elevation ■ 7460 feet
High point ■ 7460 feet
Low point ■ 6309 feet
Elevation gain ■ 1677 feet
Best hiking season ■ April through November
Maps ■ USGS Ralston Buttes
Contact ■ Jefferson County Open Space

Driving directions: There are two access points to White Ranch Park. To reach the west entry point and the beginning of our hike, drive north on Colorado 93 from Golden for 1 mile. Turn left onto Golden Gate Canyon Road and travel west for 4 miles. Turn right onto Crawford Gulch Road and follow the signs to White Ranch Park. There are two parking areas. Drive east past the first and park at the second to reach the trailhead.

Just northwest of Golden, White Ranch Park offers 18 miles of multiuse trails, many of which connect to form a variety of loops. The large ranch is home to several species of wildlife including elk, deer, mountain lions, bears, wild turkeys, and bobcats. This eastern-facing area is ideal for early morning hikes that come standard with great wildlife viewing and fantabulous sunrises. As with most Front Range hikes, White Ranch affords expansive views of some of the state's best vistas of the eastern plains.

This hike begins on the Rawhide Trail heading east toward the Longhorn Trail. From this plateau, we already have a nice view of the Mile High City—another reminder of how easy it is to access the wilderness from even the most populated areas of the state. As we wander toward the picnic area, be sure to check out the informational signs and antiquated farm equipment for more insight into the history of White Ranch—like this, for example: The year the Civil War ended, Mary and James Bond (rumor has it he equipped his horse-drawn wagons with laser-guided missiles, and his sundial watch detonated various explosives around the homestead for protection) settled in this area with the original intent of heading all the way west to California. After the death of their son, they decided to dig in and live along Colorado's Front Range. In 1913 Paul and Anna Lee White purchased some of the Bonds' land for

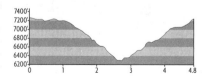

cattle ranching. Today, White Ranch is named in memory of Paul White.

The impeccably maintained trail—characteristic of all the trails in this 4000-acre open space—leads us through tall, golden grasses as it passes the picnic area where signs indicate the beginning of the Longhorn Trail. Rich fragrances of scattered ponderosa, juniper, wildflowers, wavy grasses, and yucca fill the air as we descend. Primordial hogbacks jut from the landscape like overgrown fences attempting to preserve the area from the grip of the sprawling Denver metro area. It's a peculiar sensation, trading views between Ralston Buttes to the north, then toward the city of Boulder, or between well-spaced ponderosa trees of varying height to the skyline of Denver. This parallel between nature's wonders and humanity's influence reminds us to appreciate that Colorado maintains enough outdoor savvy to

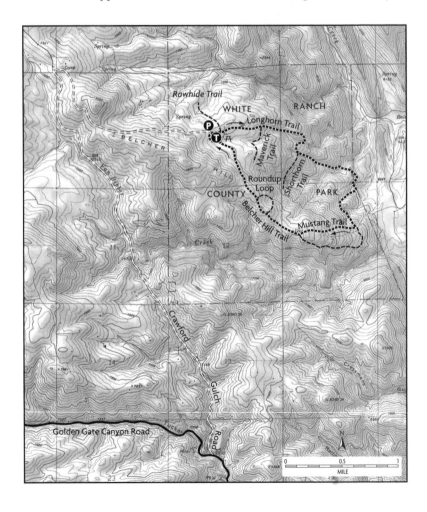

Corral on the White Ranch Trail

preserve large tracts of national forests, wilderness areas, and open space.

As we continue the descent, we stay on the Longhorn Trail, passing junctions with both the Maverick and Shorthorn Trails. Another bonus to this area is that both of these turnoffs offer shorter loop options—depending on what you're in the mood for, there are several choices to satisfy your hankering for hiking. As the elevation plunges on this east-facing mesa, the ponderosas are gradually replaced with tall grasses and low shrubbery. We'll wind south on this dusty trail and bottom out in a dry gulch. The path then abruptly ascends a switchback or two and continues tightly against the contours of the hillside. At close to 3 miles in, we pass a second junction with the Shorthorn Trail and stay on course uphill to the intersection with the Mustang Trail. Turn right onto Mustang and begin the hardest climb of the day. A small knoll offers a reprieve from the upward trudge, and from here we'll follow this ridge offering wonderful views to the north and south. Another intersection at 3.3 miles takes a right onto the Belcher Hill Trail. There is a high-backed wooden bench at this junction, perched there like a throne for the King of the Front Range. This is a good place for a quick break to enjoy views to the kingdom's far-off eastern horizon before beginning the northerly push back to the trailhead.

As customary afternoon thunderclouds take shape over the landscape, we'll quicken our step up the Belcher Hill Trail, and shoot past both the Roundup Loop and Maverick junction as this multiuse trail becomes noticeably wider through a lovely corridor of pines. At 4.1 miles, we turn right onto the Sawmill Trail, which twists into an open green meadow leading right up to the ranch. The dirt trail continues past an emergency access road and brings us back to the parking lot.

19 | LODGEPOLE LOOP

Round trip ■	**2.3 miles**
Loop direction ■	Clockwise
Hiking time ■	1 hour
Sweat factor ■	Low
Starting elevation ■	7843 feet
High point ■	8942 feet
Low point ■	7843 feet
Elevation gain ■	1508 feet
Best hiking season ■	Year-round access, but best March through October
Maps ■	USGS Conifer
Contact ■	Jefferson County Open Space

Driving directions: To reach the trailhead, drive 16 miles west of Denver on US 285. Exit onto South Turkey Creek Road, proceed under the highway and look for the Meyer Ranch trailhead signs.

Ladies and gentlemen! Boys and girls of all ages! Welcome to the greatest show on earth! According to some Jefferson County lore, this hike's history incorporates a little clowning around. Meyer Ranch Park owns some of the most appealing history in the state. Legend has it that in the 1880s, Meyer Ranch housed the animals from P. T. Barnum's circus during the winter months. Today it is not uncommon to see any number of ungulates roaming the park, but to think we are only about a century late in witnessing circus animals in the foothills of Colorado is unique indeed! The hike itself is a brief jaunt into the woods near Aspen Park and Conifer. It's a short but pleasant hike ideal for escaping the rigors of city life and enjoying refreshing woods and small dells brimming with wildflowers.

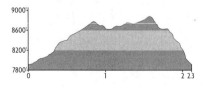

This short trip begins by winding southwest up Owl's Perch Trail past the interpretive signs at the trailhead. This wide, well-trodden trail guides itself away from the hectic populace of the freeway and delves

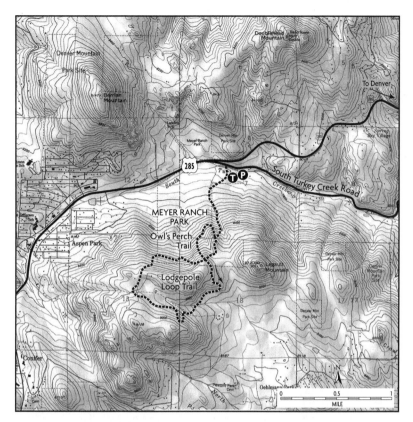

quickly into a land rich in tall grasses, wildflowers, thistle, ponderosa, and aspen. Close to a half-mile in, the Owl's Perch Trail splits temporarily, but both directions meet again shortly. Let's stay left and sneak into a nice stand of pine that quickly softens the noisy interruptions of the highway.

At the next junction, we'll continue south on the Lodgepole Loop Trail. Easy elevation gain and some lazy switchbacks guide us through this relaxing hike. Aptly named, the area is abundant with healthy lodgepole pine interspersed with spruce, fir, and an occasional ponderosa. This environment is home for a number of birds and critters like mountain bluebirds, robins, Abert's squirrels, foxes and coyotes, and deer and elk. Ambling through this pristine area, try to imagine an errant elephant or giraffe meandering through the trees! Close to 1 mile in, we'll hang right and stay on the Lodgepole Loop Trail. The trail flattens out and pleasantly wanders over small furrows and an occasional drainage.

As this peaceful hike nears its end, we'll pass the second intersection with the Sunny Aspen Trail and continue straight west. The trail turns us northeast, and after a few lazy switchbacks on the descent, we meet up with the Owl's Perch Trail again and return to the trailhead.

20 FOUNTAIN VALLEY TRAIL

Round trip ■	2.8 miles
Loop direction ■	Clockwise
Hiking time ■	1.5 hours
Sweat factor ■	Low+
Starting elevation ■	6190 feet
High point ■	6281 feet
Low point ■	6030 feet
Elevation gain ■	373 feet
Best hiking season ■	Year-round
Maps ■	USGS Kassler
Contact ■	Roxborough State Park

Driving directions: To reach the trailhead, drive south from Denver on US 85 and exit westbound on Titan Road. Follow Titan for 3.8 miles to where the road turns left and becomes North Rampart Range Road. Drive south on Rampart Range for another 3.8 miles and turn left onto Roxborough Park Road, then take an immediate right into the park.

One hundred and fifty million years ago, Roxborough State Park was a popular hangout for the likes of the massive stegosaurus, T. Rex, triceratops, and other ancient beasties. The remarkable geological formations in the park are reminiscent of those days, and hiking the Fountain Valley Trail is a trek back in time alongside enormous red ridges and slanted hogbacks dating to five hundred million years! But the laurels of this park don't stop there. As a result of the habits of wind flowing through this landscape, a number of diverse microclimates have formed, hosting a variety of flora and fauna. Roxborough is home to big critters like deer, mountain lions, bobcats, coyotes, and black bears. More than 140 species of birds have been spotted in the park, and don't forget the snakes, frogs, and even turtles. We'll pass by riparian habitats of chokecherries, wild raspberries, and Rocky Mountain maples. Porcupine, sandreed, yellow Indian, and big and little bluestem grasses wave amidst small stands of aspens, and of course, Gambel oak, Douglas-fir, ponderosa, mountain mahogany, skunkbrush, and yucca.

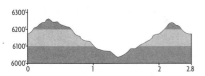

Before taking our first steps, we are treated to views of striking sandstone formations that jut harshly from the earth at gravity-defying angles. Follow the paved trail northwest away from the parking lot to the visitor center. Hikers will find a large patio with informational signs concerning the area, and packets for a self-guided tour are available from rangers.

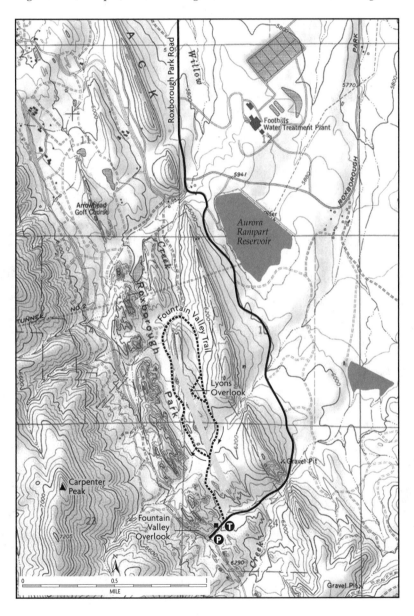

We will head northwest away from the visitor center on this wide, gravel trail, passing through a mystical grove of Gambel oak with rock spires rising above. At 0.25 mile, there is an option to branch off toward the Fountain Valley Overlook. One of two overlooks, it is well worth the time to turn left into the oak and walk up the narrow path to where a couple of benches are perched with a great view of this huge north-south hogback. Back on the main trail, we turn left at a split in the trail at 0.36 mile, and the path leads down close to the base of a long wall of red stone. The oxidation of the iron minerals within the rocks accounts for the sunset red coloration of these huge panels of rock. The trail meanders down into Fountain Valley, past large fingers of stone reaching toward the sky, and small clearings of grasses and yucca leading to the bottom of the red rock wall. Soon, walls on either side pinch this wonderfully maintained trail as we get closer to the far end of the loop. We'll cross over a small creek before cutting right and beginning our southern return, hooking around the bottom of the wall of rocks jutting up to our right. A large meadow opens up on the left where buildings from the early 1900s stand silently. We'll cross over another drainage at about 1.25 miles and begin climbing in elevation through a broad valley.

Ancient ridgeline at Roxborough State Park

At 1.7 miles, let's turn right toward the Lyons Overlook. This trail submerges into a thick stand of Gambel oak on the way up toward the second outlook on this trail. We'll pass by the split that we'll take on the return trip to the Fountain Valley Trail and continue to the top with one small switchback, making this the hardest elevation gain of the day. At the crest of this little knoll, a large platform awaits with benches and more impressive views north to the Front Range and of the large valley below. Back on the Fountain Valley Trail, turn right to continue to the top of this small valley. The trail gently curves down and makes its way back to the beginning of the loop at 2.4 miles. Now we just follow the stem back to the visitor center and trailhead.

21 EVERGREEN MOUNTAIN LOOP

Round trip ■	**4.3 miles**
Loop direction ■	Clockwise
Hiking time ■	2.5 hours
Sweat factor ■	Low+
Starting elevation ■	7480 feet
High point ■	8536 feet
Low point ■	7480 feet
Elevation gain ■	1056 feet
Best hiking season ■	March to December
Maps ■	USGS Evergreen
Contact ■	Jefferson County Open Space

Driving directions: To get here, head south on County Road 73 from Evergreen and turn west onto Buffalo Park Road. Follow the road for 1 mile to the eastern parking lot and trailhead.

Here is a short and scenic loop in Alderfer/Three Sisters Park. Located in Jefferson County Open Space near the scenic town of Evergreen, and easily accessible from Denver, too, this hike provides a nice getaway from the busy city. This 770-acre park is an ideal destination for a quick hike, with broad vistas of rolling, forested foothills, secluded trails, and glimpses out to the high reaches of the Continental Divide. Alderfer is home to the unmistakable rock formations dubbed "The Three Sisters" and "The Brother," situated in the north side of the park. Today's trail wanders through the southern section up to Evergreen Mountain.

The hike begins across the road

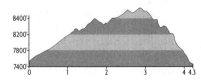

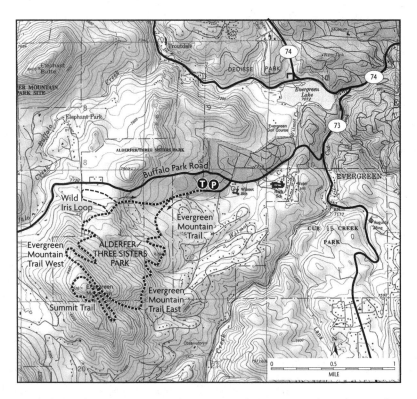

on wide, multiuse Evergreen Mountain Trail. A quarter of a mile into this landscape of ponderosa pine and meadow grasses, we will turn left toward the Evergreen Mountain Trail East, angling south toward a gradual climb. The rising elevation brings into view the rolling, wooded hills of the area, the classic Front Range prologue to the high country. As we continue to rise, we'll reach the first of a few enormous switchbacks that lead to the high point in the hike. This trail, like most in the Jefferson County Open Space system, is terrifically maintained and does a wonderful job easing hikers along the contours of the hills. The switchback hooks northwest into a shelter of pine as the trail moves in and out of the folds of Evergreen Mountain. The trail moseys a little farther west, up another switchback, and over Wilmot Creek before pushing back south.

At 1.7 miles, a nicely placed bluff rewards us with a nice spot for an early rest stop and beautiful views of the voluptuous hills embracing Evergreen. The lands of this park were first settled in 1873, and E. J. Alderfer later laid claim to the land in 1945 to raise cattle, run a sawmill, and do a little haying. The Alderfer family graciously donated much of their land to the park. Let's continue on up to the summit of the hike as the trail works its way back to the northwest. At 2.2 miles is the junction with the Summit Trail. We strongly recommend adding to the loop by heading up to the top of Evergreen Mountain for a beautiful glimpse out to the Continental Divide. From this junction, the trail becomes Evergreen Mountain Trail West and descends into dense stands of lodgepole pine on this north-facing hillside. Look and listen for a number of squirrels, chipmunks, and birds such as mountain bluebirds, red-shafted flickers, and Steller's jays. The mellow descent is made even easier by another series of switchbacks. There is evidence here of shortcutting through the woods instead of staying on the marked trail. Don't be tempted. This is a heavily used park and we can all help preserve it simply by remaining on designated trails. At 3.4 miles, there is another good opportunity to extend the trip. If you feel like adding another half-mile, take a left onto the Wild Iris Loop for a short jaunt through a small valley with more views of the mountains out west. Evergreen Mountain Trail West proceeds to the east junction of the Wild Iris Loop, and magically becomes the Ranch View Trail descending across a residential access road at 3.75 miles. From here, it is an easy stroll to the loop's first junction and a short quarter mile back to the trailhead.

22 SOUTH VALLEY PARK

Round trip ■	**2.9 miles**
Loop direction ■	Clockwise
Hiking time ■	1.5 hours
Sweat factor ■	Low
Starting elevation ■	6114 feet
High point ■	7109 feet
Low point ■	6114 feet
Elevation gain ■	1370 feet
Best hiking season ■	Year-round
Maps ■	USGS Denver
Contact ■	Jefferson County Open Space

Driving directions: To reach the trailhead from Denver, drive south on Colorado 470 and exit westbound on Ken Caryl Avenue. Turn left onto South Valley Road and drive past the northern parking area. After 2 miles, turn left at the stop sign and proceed to Deer Creek Canyon Road and make another left. Follow signs for the southern trailhead.

Just southwest of Denver lays another treasure maintained by Jefferson County Open Space. South Valley Park offers 909 acres of preserved and beautiful land close to the urban

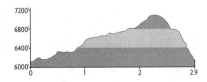

hullabaloo of the big city. We chose a couple of trails that form a lollipop loop through a valley that is home to spectacular geological formations and critical range for elk and mule deer. A number of red stone outcroppings of the Fountain and Lyons formations are scattered throughout the valley, making this short trail well worth a visit. Trail maps are available at the trailhead. One section of the loop is for hikers only; the rest of the park is multiuse. Mountain bikes and horses are common sights along the way.

This short journey begins by curving up to the north from the bottom parking lot and wrapping around a small knoll, where a massive cliff comes into view on the right. The cliff face is an enormous mural of striped rocks pocked with pine trees growing from gravity-defying locales. The well-maintained trail quickly gains elevation until it reaches the bottom of the valley. This rising plain, buttressed by the cliff, hosts an open meadow of tall grasses with red sandstone formations jutting from the ground in abrupt columns and slanting disks.

When we reach 0.4 mile, an unmarked split occurs. Let's go left here for a clockwise loop. Shortly after, we reach another junction and take a right this time toward the Swallow Trail, which begins the "hiking only" section of the trail. On nice summer weekends, South Valley Park is a popular place, so be prepared to mingle with other users. At the head of this stunning valley, a group of cottonwoods spring out of a drainage on the left as the path heads northwest up through grasses and yucca. Large curves lead past distinctive rock outcroppings. The path continues to meander uphill at a gentle pace,

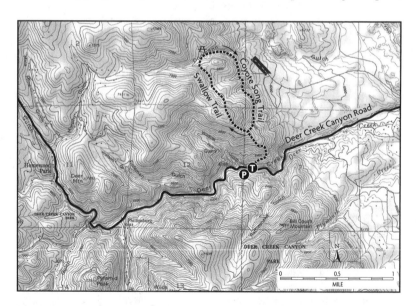

Opposite: Sandstone formations on the Swallow Trail

passing the small Mann Reservoir, and in short order we have reached the end of the Swallow Trail.

At 1.5 miles is the end of the "hiking only" trail and the junction with the northern parking lot. A number of picnic tables north of this lot provide a great place to sit and enjoy a nice summer day. The trail hooks up and around the huge outcropping dead ahead onto a well-trod clay trail leading to the Coyote Song Trail. Now on the west side and the high point of the valley, we are treated to superb views stretching down and away. The long escarpment of yellow rock traces along the narrow valley and grows in the distance to the painted wall from the beginning of the hike. In the evening, this bordering wall traps the flushed orange light of the setting sun and brightens the rocks and foliage speckling the landscape.

We will pass the junction with the Lyons Back Trail at 2.05 miles and continue heading southeast, paralleling the bottom of the cliff face. The trail gently rolls up and down and concludes the loop at 2.5 miles. One more left turn here leads back down the stem trail to the parking area.

23 GARDEN OF THE GODS

Round trip	◼ 1.5 miles
Loop direction	◼ Clockwise
Hiking time	◼ 1 hour
Sweat factor	◼ Low
Starting elevation	◼ 6455 feet
High point	◼ 6570 feet
Low point	◼ 6394 feet
Elevation gain	◼ 401 feet
Best hiking season	◼ April through October
Maps	◼ USGS Manitou Springs
Contact	◼ City of Colorado Springs Parks and Recreation

Driving directions: To reach the trailhead from Colorado Springs, follow 30th Street north from US 24, or south from Garden of the Gods Road, to the park entrance across from the visitor center. Gateway Road leads to Juniper Way Loop, a one-way road that curves left to the main parking lot. The trail begins here.

Two surveyors exploring areas south of Denver in 1859 came upon a collection of dramatic sandstone formations. One of the gentlemen

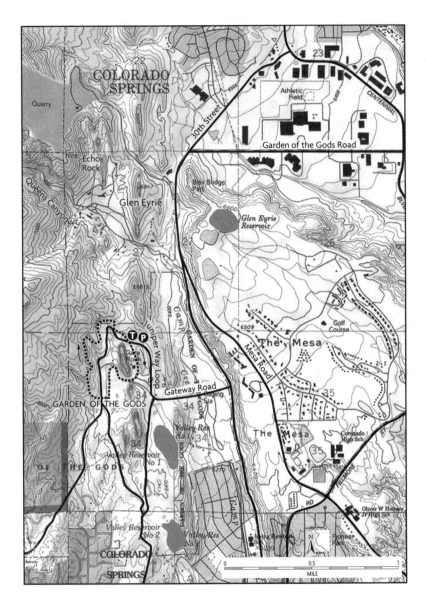

suggested it would be a "capital place for a beer garden." Fortunately, his companion had clearer vision, thinking instead "it is a fit place for the gods to assemble." So they named it Garden of the Gods, a well-chosen moniker for such a magical place. We can enjoy the enchantment thanks in large part to General William Palmer and his friend Charles Perkins. Mr. Perkins bought

One of the Gateway rocks

property in the Garden of the Gods and chose to leave his 480 acres of land in its natural state.

Our visit today follows a short trail at the north end of the park among the giant red rocks. This is a nonstrenuous hike that starts on a wide cement walking path. Weekend days find the garden brimming with people, but we're walking right next to the colossal Tower of Babel and Signature formations and there is plenty to go around. A mix of prairie grasses and mountain shrubs grow in this area, part of another fascinating feature overshadowed by the big rocks. The semiarid climate of Garden of the Gods supports an ecotone landscape, a blend of several ecosystems at the extreme limits of their range—something to keep in the back of your mind as the trail nears the passage between the imposing Gateway Rocks. There is a commons area of sorts at the base of this opening, with benches set among piñon pine and juniper. The twin spires of Sentinel Rock rise just outside of the walkways. If we curve to the right here, we'll have a nice view of the pock-marked west face of the North Gateway Rock, active with hundreds of birds flying in and out of holes and minicaves in the rock. The path hooks back to the south and meets a junction with a gravel trail heading west across the road. We have the option here to keep on the walkway and follow it past Three Graces Plaza and the Cathedral Spires back through the gateway to the trailhead for a 1-mile loop, or take this dirt trail into the thickets of ponderosa pine and juniper shrubs. The more primitive path, the Palmer Trail, sounds good; watch for traffic and cross the road to pick up the trail over there. After about 100 yards the trail makes a hard right turn and twists through low foliage and groves of ponderosa. We gained just enough elevation here to have sweet views of the majestic rock towers below: Sleeping Giant far to the south, with its keyhole window at the top, Cathedral Rock and the spires, and the two massive Gateway Rocks. Pretty cool stuff, as we wander north around a few bends at the north end of the park and back to the trailhead. An easy 1.5-mile sampler in this place fit for the gods.

Looking at a park map, you will see all kinds of dotted lines noting the location of fun trails in the garden's "backcountry." Most of them are loops, and all can be combined for whatever distance suits your fancy. There is even a mountain bike area on the eastern trails, near the Rock Ledge Ranch historic site. Spend the day and explore!

24 QUEENS CANYON

Round trip ■	3 miles
Loop direction ■	Clockwise
Hiking time ■	2.5 to 3 hours
Sweat factor ■	Low+
Starting elevation ■	6511 feet
High point ■	7644 feet
Low point ■	6507 feet
Elevation gain ■	1499 feet
Best hiking season ■	Late May through October
Maps ■	USGS Cascade
Contact ■	Pike National Forest

Driving directions: This hike is located at Glen Eyrie, just north of Garden of the Gods on 30th Street. Look for the Navigators sign and buildings between the Garden of the Gods Road and Mesa Road split. Follow the entrance road to a gatehouse, where you will be issued a permit to hike in this area. (This is private property and has been graciously opened for public use.) Once past the gatehouse, follow the road through the manicured grounds to the castle and cross a bridge to a parking lot adjacent to the castle. The trail begins at the west end of this lot at the mouth of Queens Canyon.

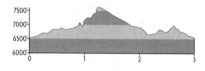

This hike truly is fit for a queen. Complete with a castle at the trailhead, this trail begins adjacent to the impeccably groomed grounds of Glen Eyrie, a Christian-based stewardship and conference center. Originally the private estate of General William Jackson Palmer in the late 1800s, the serene valley features an elegant castle available for meetings and lodging, several other outlying buildings, a carriage house, and a group camp area. All of this is tucked here and there among high canyon walls and a dreamy landscape of tidy, deep green shrubbery, stand-at-attention lawns, and vibrant flowers decorating the whole works like Christmas ornaments come to life. Best of all, Glen Eyrie is surrounded by superb hiking trails, and top on the list is Queens Canyon. This is a fantabulous trail that lazily climbs into this gorgeous canyon, following Camp Creek and high, craggy, walls. Much of the canyon is flushed with red in the stone, and it glows against the clear blue of the sky. The trail twists and bends merrily around clumps of low shrubs and small cottonwood trees, and hops over the creek again and again over stepping-stone rocks or a downed log. This means fun for us, as we explore the canyon following a wayward path, like a happy dog's footprints on a layer of newly fallen snow. A high waterfall is icing on this already sweet treat, as the trail climbs steeply to the ridge of the canyon and ambles back down through Echo Rock Canyon.

We begin our hike in the narrow opening at the bottom of a huge V, with high, red-colored walls wrinkled with cracks and perforated with holes and shallow caves. The trail meanders alongside Camp Creek and foliage in various sizes and shapes, and now and again we'll skip across the creek on small boulders or bound over it with one long stride. An unsightly water diversion pipe, which at times is actually part of the trail, buried right into the same dirt we're walking on, follows our route for a while. The pipe delivers a good share of the water from the creek, which flows from Palmer Reservoir several miles upstream, to thirsty faucets in the sprawling Colorado Springs area. This detracts from the scenery a little, but can be easily ignored as we begin to cross a series of rustic bridges over the creek. Constructed long ago of wooden planks and stout cable, these platforms grant passage over deep narrows. One notable section of bridge clings tightly to the side of the rock wall and lends the sensation it could lose its grip any second and tumble, planks, cable, and hikers all, onto the boulders below. The last bridge delivers us to the Palmer Dam, and the last time we'll see that water pipe. We should note that although Palmer's name has been affixed to typically unsavory manmade structures like dams and reservoirs, the good General was responsible for the creation or preservation of many of the special places we enjoy in this part of Colorado. Along with the other founders of Colorado Springs, General Palmer looked to future generations by setting aside large tracts of land for parks and recreational use. Even in his retirement, he presented several million dollars in gifts of parks, land, and cash donations for places like the public library and the Deaf and Blind Institute. Cheers, Mr. Palmer!

About 1 foot past the dam the trail transforms into a primitive footpath that hardly looks used. There is a fabulous feeling of seclusion as we skirt past low cedar bushes and sneak around a stand of pine. The canyon is really skinny here and the trail is littered with small boulders. It feels like the land that time forgot; every bend reveals more outstanding views, all of them complemented by that impossibly blue Colorado sky. It's quiet, too, just the soothing voice of the creek and maybe a whisper of wind in the trees. After about 1 mile we arrive at Dorothy Falls, a beautiful cascade of a 50-foot main falls with a smaller sidekick alongside. Even standing on the rocks a good distance away, you can feel mist from the falls and a wind from the force of the water.

From the falls, we'll scramble up the steep slope of loose rocks to a beauteous scene on the other side. The creek courses through a massive bowl in the canyon, betwixt stands of ponderosa pine and willow shrubs. We also have a close-up of the top of the falls as it plunges over the edge right below our

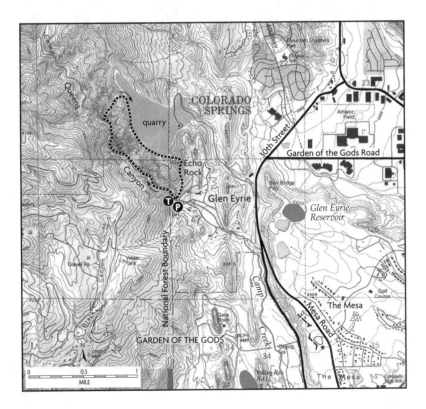

feet. Less than a half-mile farther upstream are the Punch Bowls, a cluster of glacial pockmarks in the rock. Commonly filled with water, the bowls make great pint-size swimming holes.

From our perch at the top of Dorothy Falls, look northeast to the giant—and steep—boulder field. That's our path to the top of this loop. Turn back now if you are unsure of your ability to make it up. The route

Glen Eyrie Castle

is plenty steep and there is no trail, we simply clamber over those huge boulders all the way up. The reward will be well worth the effort, though. Ready? Let's head up. Use great caution and climb staggered to avoid potential falling rock from those higher up.

After a long haul, the top of the canyon is in sight. A few more strides bring us to an open ridge devoid of trees or even shrubs of any substance. This slope is a remnant of massive mining operations that took place in the not-too-distant past. Thanks to the efforts of area residents, this hill is in the early stages of reclamation, and young trees are returning to life. As expected, great views of Colorado Springs, Black Forest, and the distant plains unfold to the east. Turn around for a spectacular sight of Queens Canyon below and Pikes Peak in the background. Our route follows the ridgeline down along an old roadbed, with nice views of the Garden of the Gods and Glen Eyrie way down there. The road curves past a former maintenance building, and here we step off the road onto a faint trail, and follow the path into the woods. A trail sign leads us down through mountain mahogany, piñon pine, and yucca. We are heading right for huge red rock needles in Echo Rock Canyon, a neighbor of Queens that shares similar beauty. As the trail nears level ground, it passes through a fun grove of Gambel oak and underneath a big cave of rock. An eye-shaped hole in the top of the cave, colored with the sky's blue, follows our progress.

The trail wanders through another tunnel of 10-foot high Gambel oak and chokecherry along a dry creekbed to an old amphitheater and parking area. We'll follow the paved road past aged buildings, take in a sweet view of the castle and grounds, and make our way back to the trailhead. What a fantastic hike.

25 THE INCLINE

		miles
L		wise
Swe		
Starting ele		
High p		
Low poin		
Elevation gain		
Best hiking season	■	
Maps	■	US
Contact	■	No C

Driving directions: To get here, follow US 24 west and exit south at Manitou Avenue. Turn left on Ruxton.

Trail closed

Ruxton to Hydro Street. A right here up the steep hill leads to the parking lot at the trailhead. If it is a weekend day, this lot will most likely be full. If that happens, head back down and park in a legal space along a nearby street. They don't hesitate to tow cars, so choose wisely.

There is a vertical scar on a hill behind Manitou Springs. The trees part in a skinny stripe littered with aged railroad ties that climb steeply to the top of this small mountain. A railroad line was constructed on this slope in 1907 to aid in construction of a hydroelectric plant, and later used to take visitors to an overlook of the town. Today, these are the proving grounds. If your competitive fire burns white hot, the Incline beckons. It will torment and punish you, then stoke that fire to come back for more. This path provides a grueling test of fitness, and unofficial record times to the top are well known and held in high regard. Just for fun, keep the number thirty in the back of your mind. Make the top under that many minutes and you can boldly brag to your buddies. Remember the feisty axiom of the Incline Club: "Go out hard. When it hurts, speed up."

From the trailhead, the well-marked Barr Trail takes off into the trees on its long haul to Pikes Peak. At the northwest corner of the parking lot, a more secluded path sneaks through low shrubbery to the top of a narrow ridge. The challenge begins here: 1.02 miles with an average grade of 41 percent, with pitches as steep as 68 percent. Looking way up there at the top of this hill, it suddenly becomes clear that this will be no picnic. Twelve hundred scruffy railroad ties embedded in dusty gravel follow an impossibly steep slope upward and out of sight. You might be looking at this trail with trepidation, maybe even fright. Or there could be a great pulse of adrenaline screaming through your body, ready to take on whatever this mountain can dish out. Take a deep breath and let's go!

The ties on this early section are mostly buried well into the ground, and are level enough to allow a nice rhythm. No big deal, right? Just like walking up a typical flight of stairs. A dozen more steps and much gasping for air tells us these stairs are different. The grade rises in a big ol' hurry, and the sweat begins to seep from our bodies just as fast. Some of the ties begin to break formation, and lie askew on the path. Many of the ties higher up are extra beefy, and some are stacked two-high. That makes for big steps and a nice burn in our quads. Before long, the trail gets so brutally steep that we have to lean way into the hill to keep from falling backward. Here and there are remnants from the track's livelier days: a rusty scrap of rail, heavy-duty spikes, and thick lines of cable plunging into solid rock like indestructible serpents. Even though your body is rapidly tiring, stay alert and use caution when selecting where to plant your next step.

Up ahead, it appears the end is near, but the mountain is only teasing us; it is a false summit and hopes of finally resting are dashed when we crest

Opposite: Steve Johnson pushes for the summit of The Incline

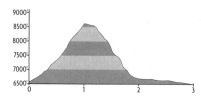

this phony peak and see the trail blast up another steep grade. Continuing this interminable ascent, you may experience a battle between physical toughness and mental tenacity. At this point in the climb, your strength streams from your face, drips off the end of your nose, and runs in salty rivulets down your arms and legs, disappearing into the dirt with your withering self-confidence. There are no breaks on this hill, no place to recover lost energy, no place to hide. So we push, retreating into ourselves and demanding our bodies to find the summit. Our efforts are rewarded as the last reaches of the trail are more manageable, and with a final burst, we're at the top. Tremendous views unveil to the east, but who cares; we're just trying to breathe, gulping in as much thin air as we can. We made it.

A faint trail wanders off to the south down a steep slope with some sections of loose gravel to connect with the Barr Trail. There are great views of the Pikes Peak cog rail cars chugging up and down the scenic valley way below as the trail bends its way around nearly one hundred switchbacks to the Barr trailhead and parking area. This is one of the shortest hikes in the book, but it packs a wallop.

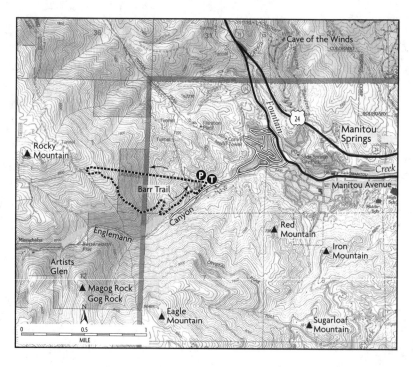

26 ┆ WALDO CANYON

Round trip ■	**6.2 miles**
Loop direction ■	Clockwise
Hiking time ■	2 to 2.5 hours
Sweat factor ■	Moderate
Starting elevation ■	7098 feet
High point ■	8190 feet
Low point ■	7098 feet
Elevation gain ■	2070 feet
Best hiking season ■	May through October
Maps ■	USGS Cascade
Contact ■	Pike National Forest

Driving directions: The trailhead for this loop is right on US 24, just over 4 miles west of Colorado Springs. Look for the brown sign with a hiker symbol that simply says, "Trail." A large turnout is available, but look for this to fill up quickly on weekends.

Waldo Canyon is a popular trail close to both Colorado Springs and Manitou Springs. It is an extremely well-constructed and maintained trail that follows the folds of the hills through groves of Gambel oak, spruce, and lodgepole pine. Elevation gain on the loop's clockwise direction is so gradual it's barely noticeable, and a couple of long stretches reveal stunning views of Pikes Peak. An excellent hike close to the city.

The trail begins by climbing a long set of stairs, then turns hard east and follows packed gravel along the canyon wall high above the traffic whizzing by on the highway. The path curves through 6-foot-tall Gambel oak, lodgepole pine, spruce, and spiny yucca at ground level. An overlook less than a half-mile in signals a left turn and the path continues its gradual ascent, passing through an arid landscape of more yucca, cactus, and a few wildflowers. It's easy walking so far, as the trail crests a short plateau with long-distance views of Colorado Springs and the eastern plains. The route then hugs the contour of the hillside into the next fold in the terrain. Ahead, a huge rock face at the head of this canyon conceals a waterfall we can hear but not see.

A short way farther along, the trail descends through a park-like setting of huge pines and monster boulders. At the bottom is a small clearing, then the trail heads uphill

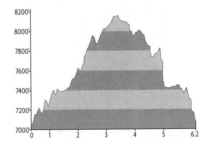

again into a stand of dense woods deep in the fold of the hill. At about 1.5 miles is the junction with the start of the Waldo Canyon Loop. Take the left fork to begin a clockwise tour of this 3.5-mile circle. A gradual ascent continues steadily along a creek to the left, up a couple of switchbacks, and across the creek into a stand of especially bright blue spruce. Giant roots from the trees lie across the trail like petrified serpents, and tiny purple flowers at trail's edge abruptly take off and flutter away—they're butterflies after all. The trail crosses the creek twice more and climbs a steeper grade past some big ol' rock formations, breaking free of the trees to reveal

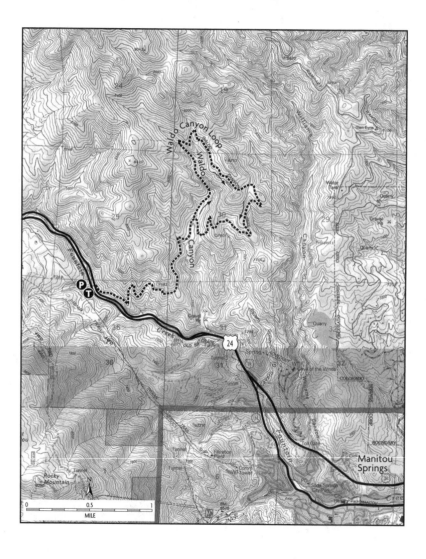

Waldo Canyon

a stop-in-your-tracks view of Pikes Peak to the southwest, along with its shorter neighbor, Sheep Mountain. Cross into another pleat in the hill and into a thick stand of pines and one more creek. About 3 miles in, the scenery changes with just a few steps to grassy foliage and a clear understory beneath huge pines, with a tread of packed dirt. Curving south, the trail descends steadily on loose shale to a couple of switchbacks that soon point the path directly at Sheep Mountain.

We are trekking on dolomite, sandstone, and limestone in this area, all of which was once beneath a massive ocean. It's hard to imagine that this cactus and yucca, and of course these big hills, used to be under water. Even the granite of Pikes Peak was once molten rock 20 miles below the earth's surface. The trail descends into a canyon, up over a small hill, then switchbacks down in a hurry to 4.5 miles and the junction with the start of the loop. Your legs can tell you that the counterclockwise choice with this loop dishes out a pretty good climb right off the bat. From here, follow the trail back south and west to the stairs, and down to the trailhead.

27 | LOVELL GULCH TRAIL

Round trip ■	**5 miles**
Loop direction ■	Counterclockwise
Hiking time ■	2.5 to 3 hours
Sweat factor ■	Low+
Starting elevation ■	8620 feet
High point ■	9326 feet
Low point ■	8620 feet
Elevation gain ■	951 feet
Best hiking season ■	June through October
Maps ■	USGS Mount Deception
Contact ■	Pike National Forest

Driving directions: To reach the trailhead from Woodland Park and US 24, head north on Baldwin, which curves into Rampart Range Road. The trailhead is 2 miles north on the left. Look for the Lovell Gulch Trail sign.

Here is a relaxing hike on a lollipop trail looping through a nice mix of native trees, large granite boulders, small valleys, and a ridge affording views of Pikes Peak and the Sawatch Range. One long climb will stretch legs and lungs a bit; otherwise grades and crowds are moderate on this quiet trail. Woodland Park is right down the road with all kinds of eateries, shops, and other distractions. Rampart Reservoir is only a few extra miles east, with more trails and opportunity for water-related activities.

The Lovell Gulch Trail starts at the gate and follows loose gravel past a roads maintenance facility and a big water tank, then climbs gently though a thin pine and aspen forest. The landscape is relatively arid and the trail wanders through grassy areas over a ridge into thicker woods and a creek crossing into Lovell Gulch and the junction with the main loop at 1 mile. Let's turn right here to start the 3.75-mile loop, following the creek and a narrow riparian ribbon at the edge of the trees. The north slope of the gully is a meadow of tall grasses with a spattering of tall ponderosa pine and a stray boulder here and there. The trail climbs a barely noticeable grade to around the 1.5-mile mark, where it bends north. A little farther along, it leads into

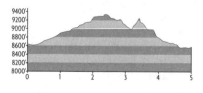

a small collection of huge granite boulders amidst a grove of aspen, offering adventurous scrambling or a pleasant rest stop. From here, the trail starts to get a bit more serious about going uphill, and a couple

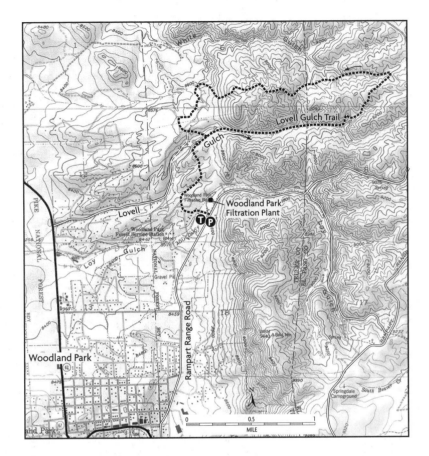

of moderate switchbacks lead to a plateau next to Rampart Range Road. We go west from here, following a ridge guided by powerlines overhead. Try to look away from the manmade distraction and instead enjoy the fine views west toward the fourteeners of the Collegiate Peaks, or Pikes Peak reigning over the tops of the forest below. A steady descent is followed by a long, steep climb that peaks at a plateau with a superb view of the aforesaid mountains and Woodland Park below.

A steep descent slippery with loose rock takes us to the third mile, where the trail slices through the contour lines of the landscape. Soon, the grade becomes more gradual and we wander into another aspen stand. Pikes Peak dominates the view directly ahead, and the trail parallels quiet pasture to the west. The junction with the stem of the loop is right over the next small rise, and we just have to retrace the path back to the trailhead and almost 5 miles for the day.

Boulders on Lovell Gulch Trail

28 ¦ CHEESMAN RANCH

Round trip ■	**12 miles**
Loop direction ■	Counterclockwise
Hiking time ■	6 hours
Sweat factor ■	High
Starting elevation ■	9698 feet
High point ■	9698 feet
Low point ■	9210 feet
Elevation gain ■	536 feet
Best hiking season ■	Late May through October
Maps ■	USGS Divide
Contact ■	Mueller State Park

Driving directions: To reach Mueller State Park, follow US 24 west from Colorado Springs to Divide, then head south on Colorado 67 for just over 3 miles to the park entrance. A daily park pass will make us $5 lighter, and the main road winds 1.5 miles to the Elk Meadow trailhead.

Mueller State Park boasts more than 55 miles of trails laced throughout its 5000 acres of rolling woods and meadows. With the immense west face of Pikes Peak as a backdrop, hikers can get way out there and wander remote areas of the park, or take a quiet stroll on a short loop near the campground. Elk, black bears, eagles, hawks, and a lot of other wildlife are commonly seen throughout the park. This trail starts right out with panoramic views of Pikes Peak, follows rolling terrain through meadows and aspen glades, and concludes with deep woods in secluded valleys. Highlights of the hike are the original Cheesman Ranch property and buildings along the trail, and great views of the Sangre de Cristo Range.

The trail system in Mueller State Park is organized by numbers. Our route today starts on Trail 18 at the Elk Meadow parking lot and trailhead. The wide trail (accessible to hikers, bikers, and horses) plunges quickly into stands of ponderosa and lodgepole pine interspersed with ubiquitous aspen groves. Throughout the hike, various fire access roads break off the trail so be sure to stay true to the desired path. Close to 0.5 mile, the trail twists north and the best views of Pikes Peak begin to appear. There are plenty of options to rest and gaze up at the 14,000-foot mountain, buttressed by a speckled blanket of the aforementioned pine and aspen. In the fall, these lower flanks are lit with gold for an even more impressive sight. The trail continues

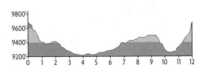

to roll up and down, in and out of closed-in woods and open, sprawling meadows. We'll pass a junction with Trail 19 and after about 2 miles, the trail turns into Trail 17, the Cheesman Ranch Trail, which follows a mellow course north out onto a huge plain bordered on the right by a crowded line of trees and Colorado 67. The trail soon curves away from the highway to a junction with Trail 33. We'll continue on Trail 17 past an old crumbling cabin and begin a descent through an aspen grove. As the trail bottoms out near a creek, it passes the original Cheesman farmstead, complete with the old log home, a barn and corral, and even the outhouse. A split rail fence outlines the property and the place looks remarkably authentic.

The path continues to roll over small hills along the creek, with pine woods on our left and a grassy meadow on our right. As the trail enters the trees, it begins a long, sustained climb for an entire mile to the junction with Trail 32. Our route remains with Trail 17, so follow the right turn arrow for a short distance to the junction with Trail 12, the Homestead Trail, just

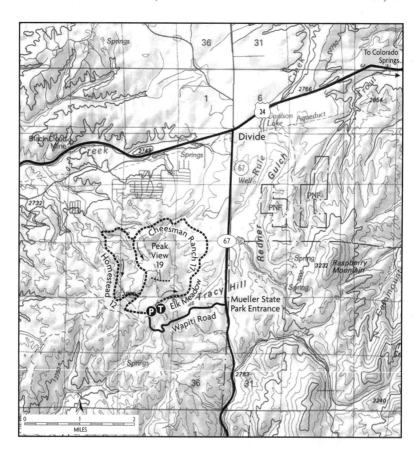

before reaching the parking area. Take Trail 12 down into a sunken meadow, followed by a quiet riparian zone bordered by dense pine forest. A junction with Trail 31 comes along, but we'll stay on course with Trail 12, making a hard right and crossing through the swamp and over the creek to a huge climb up to the junction with Trail 13. Head straight ahead on 12, downhill this time into a serene, forested valley.

The path rolls up and down for a bit, then hits us with a long and steep climb that gets even steeper at the top before reaching the park road at the Homestead trailhead around 7.5 miles. From here, it's a right turn and an easy cool-down stroll along the road back to the Elk Meadow trailhead.

29 ┊ BEAVER CREEK LOOP

Round trip	■	**6.9 miles**
Loop direction	■	Clockwise
Hiking time	■	4.5 hours
Sweat factor	■	Moderate+
Starting elevation	■	5955 feet
High point	■	7436 feet
Low point	■	5950 feet
Elevation gain	■	1486 feet
Best hiking season	■	Year-round
Maps	■	USGS Phantom Canyon
Contact	■	Bureau of Land Management

Driving directions: From Canon City, follow Highway 50 east for 6 miles. Turn left (north) onto Phantom Canyon Road (County 67) and drive 1.6 miles to County 123. Turn right and drive 0.25 mile to Beaver Creek Road (County 132) and turn left. Follow this road for 11 miles to the trailhead at the end of the road.

Here is a fun hike in the 27,000-acre Beaver Creek Wilderness Study Area. Rugged mountains, an incredible diversity of plant and animal life, and a beautiful rushing creek highlight this loop. The trail offers big climbs and long descents, and the end of the trail quietly follows a gulch filled with huge trees, high canyon walls, and a peppering of wildflowers. This area also boasts one of the richest wildlife habitats in Colorado, including one of the greatest concentrations of mountain lions in the state. Keep your eyes peeled for the likes of

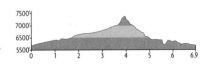

bighorn sheep, mule deer, elk, black bear, and bobcat, as well. Skies above are graced with peregrine falcons, hawks, and eagles.

From the parking area, we'll walk northeast along a wide road lined with a chain of cottonwoods and willows. As we get closer to Beaver Creek, there

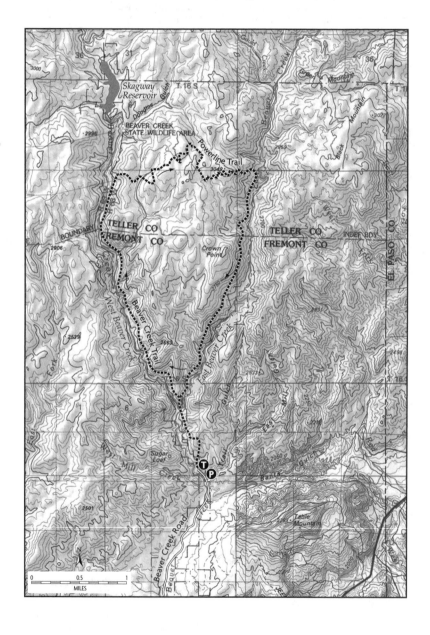

Butterfly (Photo by Sierra Overlie)

is a beautiful sandstone knoll speckled with juniper and piñon, and to the left is a canvas of bucolic farmland. The sandy double-track road hooks around this small knoll to a left turn at the first junction at 0.25 mile. A little farther north, we will approach the flanks of the creek, flowing with fervor from the high reaches of Pikes Peak. A rocky, arid wall of juniper and piñon makes up the right side of this corridor, while the water-loving cottonwoods and willows trail off on the left. We'll cross the stream at 0.7 mile. With no bridge, the crossing can be a little tricky, and cold, especially in the spring. Shed the boots and socks, roll up the pants, and wade into the knee-deep icy runoff to cross over to the other side.

On the other side, the Beaver Creek Trail switchbacks hard to the left and steeply rises above the riverbed. The path travels into a landscape dominated by Gambel oak and ponderosa pine as it follows the contours of this canyon wall, with terrific views of the curving creek and the canyon system throughout. Farther north, tall, striated cliff faces overlook the entire area. Numerous social trails branch off to various camp spots, oftentimes still equipped with unsightly fire pits. Do your best to stay on the main path on the right side of the creek, which stays above the creek for about 2 miles before dropping down to it once again. And keep your eyes peeled here. This seldom-traveled area is home to one of the higher concentrations of mountain lions in Colorado. The trail winds up and down to a confluence of the east and west forks of Beaver Creek. At 3.2 miles, we turn right onto the Powerline Trail. Compared to the mellow gradients thus far, this section of trail climbs steeply through oak, Douglas-fir, and even some Engelmann spruce now and again. It is a sharp and at times downright arduous climb up these switchbacks toward the high point in the loop.

Just past 4 miles, the trail summits and we receive our first views of the eastern portion of the Beaver Creek Wilderness and the flats out south. Look aloft for elegant raptors soaring the currents. A squirrelly descent takes us down more switchbacks through a landscape similar to that of the ascent. At 4.5 miles, we reach the bottom of the steep climb and find the habitually dried out Trail Gulch, which marks our return path. The trail heads south, crisscrossing over the gulch a number of times. The canyon walls close in and open up and close again, featuring a lot of cacti, yucca, ponderosa, juniper, and piñon pine. Steep walls on either side make the canyon narrow at times and caution should be exercised during periods of heavy rain. It is not uncommon for flash floods to rip through this area during spring. Soon, the sounds of Beaver Creek come back into earshot as we approach the end of this hike. The trail makes one more small climb and now we can see the valley leading to the trailhead. At 6.6 miles, we reach the initial junction with the Beaver Creek Trail and the close of the loop. A left turn on the short stem trail arrives at the parking area to close this lovely hike.

30 PUEBLO MOUNTAIN PARK

Round trip ■	2.8 miles
Loop direction ■	Counterclockwise
Hiking time ■	1.5 to 2 hours
Sweat factor ■	Low+
Starting elevation ■	6746 feet
High point ■	7271 feet
Low point ■	6676 feet
Elevation gain ■	1008 feet
Best hiking season ■	May through October
Maps ■	USGS Beulah
Contact ■	San Isabel National Forest

Driving directions: To reach the Pueblo Mountain Park, drive southwest on County Road 78 (South Pine Drive) from Pueblo for 25 miles into the town of Beulah. Stay left on County Road 78 where the road forks and proceed 3 miles to the entrance of the park on the right. Stay left at each intersection to reach the Mountain Park Environmental Center; go past the MPEC and up to the northern end of the park to the Devils Canyon trailhead and picnic area.

Pueblo Mountain Park is a small haven residing right between the city of Pueblo and the Sangre de Cristo Range. Home to 611 acres of land in the Wet Mountains, the park offers more than 6 miles of trails exploring this wonderfully rich and diverse area. This hike takes us past a rushing creek, onto open hillocks covered with cacti, yucca, ponderosa, and juniper, and deep into moist valleys of fir trees and wildflowers. The trail also summits a high lookout atop a rocky overlook granting views of the nearby town of Beulah and out to the eastern plains of southern Colorado. The hike isn't complete, however, without a stop at the Mountain Park Environmental Center near the entrance of the park. The MPEC's friendly staff offer a number of educational activities, including guided interpretive hikes, school programs, summer nature camps, and a variety of nature workshops and lectures. Be sure to check it out!

This leisurely hike begins by moving northwest from the trailhead on a well-maintained dirt trail, descending rapidly down to the creek slivering through Devils Canyon and a world made up of Gambel oak, Douglas-fir, and ponderosa pine. The creek owes its fantastic name, Devils Dribble, to its variable water levels. In the spring, we find it rushing at capacity—a main artery giving life to the foliage in the area. But come late summer, this creek is truly reduced to a dribble, the majority of which flows underground! We'll wander into this gulch and cross over the creek to a junction, where we'll turn right and saunter along the North Ridge Trail. The hard-packed red dirt and clay trail makes for easy strolling past more groves of oaks and conifers. The trail quickly turns back to the northwest revealing nice views on our right of one of the valleys in the beautiful town of Beulah, with wide fields, stables, and a stock arena.

Continuing west now, we begin a long journey upward on a series of switchbacks, initially rising through huge, robust ponderosa with a lovely understory of softer fir and spruce. But as the trail wanders over to the sun-splashed, south-facing side of the mounting hill, the trees give way to spiky yuccas, claret cup cacti, jumbled rocks and an occasional juniper. The songs of the creek echo up through the beautiful, rocky walls that create Devils Canyon, and with higher elevations come even better views of rural Beulah. At about 0.65 mile, we finish the most significant switchbacks and stroll across a flat area with the reemergence of dense trees dropping down the hillside on our right. Look carefully into those trees for glimpses of some of the wide variety of birds

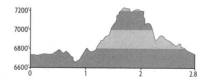

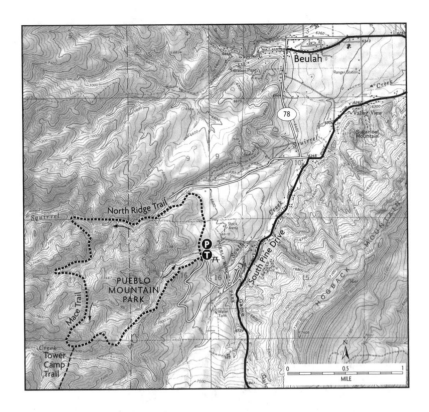

that make their homes in the park, like the white-breasted nuthatch, Cooper's hawks, western tanagers, American dippers, and even the reclusive flammulated owl.

After the short flat, we'll continue to climb back into the woods, following another small drainage for a while before topping out at 1 mile at the next junction. A right turn provides deep access into the San Isabel National Forest. Let's explore that avenue another day and instead turn left onto the North Ridge Trail. The trail descends atop a ridge with delightful views west of the rolling hills of the forest, and broad vistas east of scattered homes far off on the eastern plains. From here, a couple of long switchbacks plunge the trail down into the pines again as we make our way to the head of Devils Canyon. The arid landscape gives way to the cool, shadowed, fir-dominated canyon of the creek. Another small creek rambles down to the valley floor here and the trail continues its quick descent. At 1.6 miles, the trail hits the floor and crosses Devils Dribble before turning right and heading south into another fantastic valley. Come springtime, a number of colorful accents add to the scene, including Nelson larkspur, pasque flowers, spring beauties, and sugarbowls.

Ivy at Pueblo Mountain Park

The path hops back and forth across the creek and at 1.7 miles the North Ridge Trail ends and is picked up by the Mace Trail, which banks hard left and quickly rises away from the gurgling creek. At 1.8 miles, continue straight on the Mace Trail past the junction with the Tower Camp Trail. Just ahead, let's break off toward Lookout Point. The trail winds up around a knoll and reaches the rocky bluff that certainly earns its name. The best views of the day are granted here of the rolling topography in this fantastic little valley community. Well, the hike is nearly over, so let's enjoy the sun, the smell of the arid ponderosas, the views of the plains out east, and this deeply gorged canyon below our feet for a bit longer, then move back down to the Mace Trail, turn left, and complete this pleasant hike. One more big arc and a couple of gentle switchbacks lead us back northeast through the oak and pine, all the way back to the picnic area and trailhead.

31 PETRIFIED FOREST LOOP

Round trip ■	**1.5 mile**
Loop direction ■	Clockwise
Hiking time ■	45 minutes
Sweat factor ■	Low
Starting elevation ■	8360 feet
High point ■	8400 feet
Low point ■	8330 feet
Elevation gain ■	80 feet
Best hiking season ■	Year-round
Maps ■	USGS Lake George
Contact ■	Florissant Fossil Beds National Monument

Driving directions: To get to the Florissant Fossil Beds National Monument, drive west out of Colorado Springs on US 24 for 34 miles to the town of Florissant. Turn left (south) onto County Road 1 and drive 2.5 miles to the turnoff for the visitor center. All trails begin at the back door of the visitor center.

When a settler from Missouri came to the site of present-day Florissant, he was so taken with its beauty that he named it after his hometown. Florrisant is French for "flowering," and this town is indeed home to vibrant rolling meadows, forests, and a variety of wildlife. While you might see a coyote, mountain lion, golden eagle, or mountain bluebird here today, the scene was a tad different 35 million

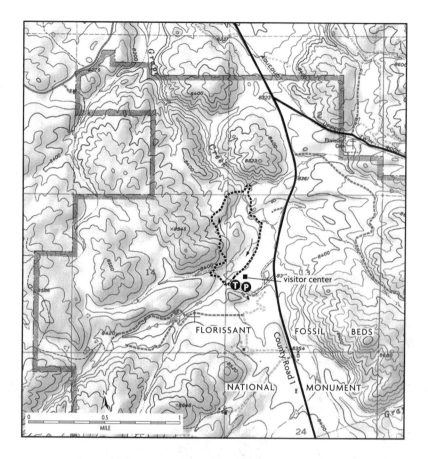

years ago. Instead of coyotes and cougars, Heptodons and Coryphodons, early ancestors of the modern horse, might have been spotted in this area. Instead of aspens and ponderosas, cattails would have grown out of the huge lake that formerly occupied this space, and monster redwood trees also grew in the swampy climate. This short and easy hike boasts amazing remains of the aforesaid ancient redwood trees, and the visitor center hosts a variety of fossilized insects, leaves, and fish. The park also offers a number of guided tours, seminars, and even junior ranger programs.

A short walk on the half-mile Walk Through Time loop first guides visitors to a sheltered amphitheater protecting a few massive sequoia stumps. Huge redwood trees, like those in California, stood hundreds of feet tall among oak, maple, and hickory neighbors. The lake was full of fish and the damp atmosphere attracted thousands of small insects and a variety of birds. Hard to believe on a hot August day at around 8000 feet, but the tale is true nonetheless. This short path also features a small shale outcropping that bears fossils of small insects. The best of these fossils, however, are preserved in the visitor center. Caterpillars, wasps, and spiders are just some of the critters delicately preserved in stone for some 35 million years.

The Petrified Forest Loop branches off from the Walk Through Time trail and wanders north through tall grasses and large ponderosas with the beautiful ridges of Pikes Peak providing a backdrop. It takes us on a well-maintained path through some trees and down to the "Big Stump." The remains of this impressive chunk of tree owe their existence to ancient volcanoes that once occupied this area. Only the stoutest of trees, like this one here, were able to withstand the velocity of the mud and ash flooding from the eruptions. Over the last 35 million years, the casings of this volcanic mud have slowly turned the bases of these sequoias into petrified tree stumps. From here, the trail eases east before cruising back south toward the parking area, passing more remnants of ancient and massive trees. On our Walk Through Time and Petrified Forest Loops, we will cover only about 1.5 miles, but this park hosts 14 miles of trails, most of which are in loops. The Hornbek Wildlife Loop, the Boulder Creek Trail, and the Hans Loop provide more meadows, trees, rock outcroppings, and wonderful vistas. Florrisant is the perfect place to study our long-ago history.

Massive petrified Sequoia stump

CENTRAL MOUNTAINS

32 | FANCY PASS TRAIL

Round trip	■	**8.5 miles**
Loop direction	■	Counterclockwise
Hiking time	■	5 to 6 hours
Sweat factor	■	Moderate+
Starting elevation	■	10,090 feet
High point	■	12,390 feet
Low point	■	10,007 feet
Elevation gain	■	2584 feet
Best hiking season	■	Late June through October
Maps	■	USGS Mount of the Holy Cross
Contact	■	White River National Forest

Driving directions: To reach the trailhead, follow US 24 north from Leadville or south from Minturn to Forest Road 703, and head southwest along scenic Homestake Creek for 8 miles. Turn right onto Forest Road 704 and continue 3 miles to the trailhead. Register at the kiosk, take along the supplied wilderness permit, and head for the hills.

This trail lives up to its name with gusto. We could hardly ask for a more spectacular setting, with the consistently beautiful Sawatch Range to the west and the high peaks of the Continental Divide and the Tenmile and Mosquito Ranges east. This hike is one of the prettiest in the state, with no intermission in this concert of rugged mountains, high alpine lakes, cascading streams, and immense glacial valleys here in the southern reaches of the Holy Cross Wilderness. A steep initial climb leads to Fancy Pass, then down into the bucolic Missouri Lakes area and a return along Missouri Creek. A fancy hike, indeed.

The trail begins on hard-packed tread with freckles of rocks as it delves into a quiet forest mix of lodgepole pine, spruce, and subalpine fir. Climbing gradually, we enter the Holy Cross Wilderness and just ahead are a couple of steep switchbacks and some nice views of the mountains of the Divide to the east.

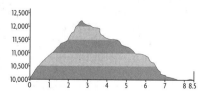

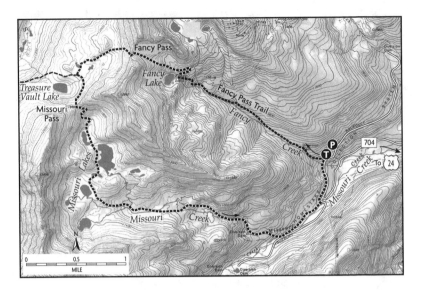

This wilderness area is loaded with alpine lakes and streams, more than twenty-five peaks rising above 13,000 feet, and the namesake for the wilderness, Mount of the Holy Cross. The pretty stream to our right is Fancy Creek, and the trail passes through tranquil settings of wildflowers and riparian gardens colored soggy green. Farther along, a log bridge crosses the creek to softer tread with roots and stumps, while breaks in the trees reveal great views of the Holy Cross Ridge just ahead. After a couple of bends in the trail, we come upon a beauteous sight: a deep, rugged gorge sliced into the rock carries the squiggly stripe of the creek down toward Homestake Creek. The narrow V reaches way up the hill and out of sight, and the trail follows a series of steep switchbacks to a small overlook providing a look over the edge to enjoy the view of the gorge from up high.

A few dozen steps later, the trees become sparse as we near tree line. The grade has been steady and often steep since the start, but a few flat sections along the way gave our legs a chance to recover. On the other hand, even if the trail climbed straight up, the scene unfolding over that next rise will take your mind off all manner of tired lungs and legs. Nestled in the embrace of a half moon of mountains, Fancy Lake's placid waters reflect a landscape of deep green pines and moss-covered boulders on a grassy knoll, wildflowers all over the place, and inquisitive rainbow trout swimming just offshore. There is a petite waterfall on the rocks across the lake where Fancy Creek begins its journey. It is truly an elegant sight, and a nice place to take a nap, or just linger a bit, or even pitch a tent and enjoy an overnighter just 2 miles from the trailhead.

Tear yourself away from this beautiful place and follow the path up around the lake, staying with the sign for Fancy Pass Trail. The grade is significantly steeper now, with a lot of rocks en route. There is a great view of the lake below and the mountain ranges way off to the east. This is rugged country, with a raw and untamed feel, but stunning all the same. Marmots and pikas scamper about the rocks, scolding as we pass over sections of scree to arrive at the top of Fancy Pass at 12,390 feet. Wow. We gained nearly 3000 feet in just over 2 miles. It was tough, but what a reward this is. Decadent views stretch as far as we can see in every direction. Two lakes appear as mere puddles below the pass, there are scores of big thirteeners everywhere, and dots of water in far-off tarns are tucked among the hills, along with snowfields and panoramic views of Holy Cross Ridge and the Sawatch Range. Nice!

From the pass, the trail descends toward Treasure Vault Lake. Our boots

Missouri Creek in deep gorge

spring merrily on spongy tread where rivulets and creeks run through grasses into an exquisite basin of wildflowers and expansive rock fields. A junction with the trail leading west to Blodgett Lake and the trail heading south and uphill again to Missouri Pass appears at about the 4-mile mark. Our route goes southbound, so follow the path up another climb, this time much more gradual than the first, to Missouri Pass at 11,900 feet. Below is a huge U-shaped valley of steep cliffs and high ridges, and way down there are the Missouri Lakes, a collection of a dozen pristine mountain lakes surrounded by groves of spruce and fir. We descend toward this Eden over rocky tread, past boulders and renegade foliage in the harsh landscape near the pass. The scene at the bottom is just as we expected: lichen-covered rock amid piñon pine and fir, and clear, quiet lakes surrounded by dramatic mountains. This is a likely place to spot wildlife, too, like deer, lynx, elk, bobcats, and black bears, and streams are loaded with trout. We'll stroll through a grove of pine along the edge of one of the lakes, top out over a hill, and continue descending back to tree line. The trail crosses Missouri Creek a couple of times and passes some scenic waterfalls and a wetland area loaded with flowers. Soon the path descends steeply to another deep, narrow gorge like the one on the other side. This one is equally dramatic, and even skinnier up on top; you could almost jump across parts of this slender canyon. The creek roars underneath a bridge and out of sight around a bend. Farther ahead, we meet the creek again, but now it lazily riffles over logs and rocks and is perfect company along the trail. The grade levels as we near the bottom of the valley and the creek deposits itself into a small lake, which dumps over a 30-foot waterfall in dramatic fashion. From here, the trail parallels the creek again to follow a forest road back to the trailhead.

33 ┆ MOUNT OF THE HOLY CROSS

Round trip ▪	**15 miles**
Loop direction ▪	Clockwise
Hiking time ▪	11+ hours
Sweat factor ▪	High++
Starting elevation ▪	10,315 feet
High point ▪	14,005 feet
Low point ▪	9841 feet
Elevation gain ▪	6790 feet
Best hiking season ▪	Late June through October
Maps ▪	USGS Mount of the Holy Cross
Contact ▪	White River National Forest

Driving directions: The trail begins at the Half Moon Pass campground. Take US 24 to Tigiwan Road (Forest Road 707), about halfway between

Minturn and Red Cliff. Follow this road for eight twisty, bumpy miles to the campground. There is a separate parking area for day use.

This second hike in the Holy Cross Wilderness is a challenging pilgrimage to the summit of Mount of the Holy Cross. It is a tough day hike on steep grades and long stretches of trailless bouldering, but it is also one of the most rewarding hikes in the entire state. There are unforgettable views of the namesake mountain and its trademark cross, demanding scrambles up a succession of thirteener peaks and a fourteener peak, and a deep valley descent. A truly epic day is in store. Bring plenty of food and water and a good map, plan on an alpine start (at least 3 am), and set aside about 11 hours to complete the loop.

From the trailhead, we will follow the Fall Creek Trail to the left and behind the information sign. Remember this trail from the Fancy Pass hike (Hike 32)? This is the other end of the path coming down from Fancy Pass. A short bridge crosses Notch Mountain Creek and the trail jumps right into a dense lodgepole and spruce forest. The grade is steady on hard-packed tread with rocks and roots, but it's gradual, just right to warm up the lungs and legs for what is to come. In about a half-mile, we pass a huge talus slide and there are nice views east to the mountains of the Continental Divide and the Tenmile Range. At 2 miles is the junction with the Notch Mountain Trail. The path is narrow and rocky here, with a couple of steep switchbacks right off the bat, and those views to the east are getting better, with the mountains backlit by the early glow of the sunrise. The forest thins as tree line nears, and the trail winds into a rocky landscape mixed with green grasses and small thickets of spruce and fir scattered among rock gardens of wildflowers and other pretty foliage. The path ducks in and out of the trees toward the big, rugged cliffs of Notch Mountain looming above. Sweeping views showcase the deep valley way below. Keep climbing up and up about 1.5 miles to an open saddle at 13,000 feet, just below Notch Mountain, and behold the incredible sight of Mount of the Holy Cross in all its glory. 'Tis a breathless view of the famous mountain and its rugged couloirs. Our early start got us to this point at sunrise, and what a sight it is, with the sun bathing the summit and the entire cross in fresh orange and yellow. That small knob of a summit is our goal for the day. Between here and there is a huge basin of mountains with a frigid lake at the bottom. This is the Bowl of Tears, a gnarly ridgeline with knife-edge drops arcing around to the Holy Cross. It's a rugged, daunting place, but beautiful all the same. It commands respect with just a cursory glance, and guess what? That's our route! We'll travel all the way around this basin, on no trail, with three successively higher thirteeners en route, just to reach the saddle below Holy Cross. Next comes the final ascent. Yikes. Before

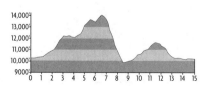

we get to the tough part of the hike, let's take a break in the sturdy rock-walled shelter here. The shelter is complete with a brawny wooden door, fireplace, and a huge table set in front of a row of windows overlooking that amazing view—this is a perfect place to replenish our stores.

Take a deep breath and let's go. We'll cross this short "flat" section from the shelter and climb the first boulder slope, a jumble of big, angular rocks hued lime green with lichen. Use great caution from here on out; these rocks offer plentiful chances to twist or break an ankle or leg. If a rock sounds hollow, beware. Step off and pick another one. If it's raining, think twice about being up here at all; the lichen and moss on the rocks turns greasy, making it nearly impossible to retain any kind of grip.

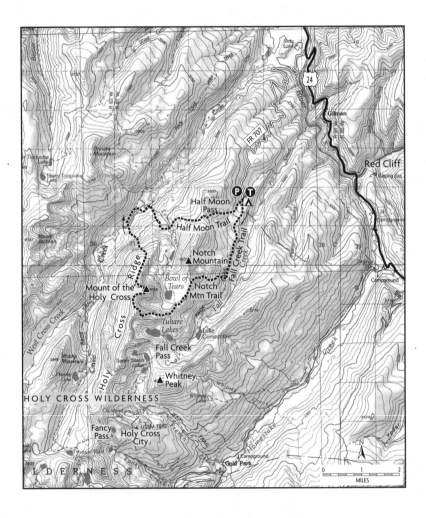

Shelter on saddle below Notch Mountain

Finally at the top of this first unnamed peak, at 13,248 feet, we can see our charge for the next few hours: up one mountain, down the saddle, up the next one, down, up, down. Whew. Scrambling down, we reach the first saddle, just a skinny path with steep slopes on one side and just plain scary, precipitous cliffs dropping 1000 feet into the basin on the other. It feels truly wild out here, so utterly and willingly exposed to nature. We have a great view of Lake Constantine and the Fall Creek valley below, and the high peaks of the Continental Divide to the southeast. The saddle is part of a huge, east-facing cirque, and we'll follow it almost halfway around to where it blends into the next big hill. This second climb is tough, over more big boulders on a steeper grade than the first. At the top, standing at 13,373 feet, look southwest over an ocean of rugged peaks all the way to the horizon. Look any other direction and see more of the same. This is what it's all about. There is a great view of Tuhare Lakes below, separated by a gorgeous waterfall, and a massive cirque enclosure of vertical cliffs.

The descent from peak number two is gradual, and the next saddle is almost flat heading over to the last climb. Again, there are huge drops on both sides, especially to our right, where the earth plunges over 1000 feet in about four steps. Check out Whitney Peak, Middle Mountain, and scores of others to the south and west, and of course the peak with the cross right over there to the north. The last climb to the third mountain is tougher yet, with several false summits to tease us, but the biggest hill of all is in sight and that drives us on. Good thing, because the drop down to the final saddle is steep and technical and robs us of already dwindling energy. There is a terrifying drop to the east with cornices of snow concealing certain death should you decide to walk over there. The ground to the west slopes rapidly away and disappears 2000 feet into a narrow valley with Cross Creek at the bottom. We're on our way now to the final ascent to Mount of the Holy Cross. From this approach, we are forced to tackle a monstrous boulder field, but this time we have the luxury of a handful of cairns to lead the way. Before long we meet what serves as a trail up the homestretch. At long last, we have made it to the summit at 14,005 feet. Wow. The views are simply stunning. We can see the Vail ski area, the Gore Range, the string of peaks of the Holy Cross Ridge, and the Sawatch Range. If you look closely, you can see Mount Elbert, the highest point in the state, far to the south. Above it all is that perfect Colorado sky, so clear and deep blue, it looks like you could reach right into it and touch your daydreams. The mountain itself also inspires, albeit in a more frightening sense. Walk very carefully over to the eastern edge and gaze down into the depths of the main couloir. The abyss below feels alive; it reaches right into your head and tugs at your fears, mostly those of falling for a really long time. It would definitely be the last step you'd take, so take it easy up here.

After enjoying a high-altitude break, it's time to get down before an afternoon thunderstorm decides to show up. Head back down the boulder slope and follow the path north along a long ridgeline between Cross Creek and East Cross Creek. Going downhill is no picnic, either, with more big boulders and a steep grade with nary a switchback to be had, but there are great views of Cross Creek way down there, along with a few waterfalls on the slopes west of the creek. The descent is long and arduous, but we finally reach a trail and leave the boulders behind. It's still a long way to the bottom and the steep grade makes for tough going. The true valley floor arrives after hiking forever in the woods. It is quite beautiful down here as we traverse East Cross Creek and hop over a small hill. Don't get too comfortable, though, because the big mountain in front of us is the one we walk over to get back to the trailhead. And this one is difficult, too, as the path, Half Moon Trail, climbs steeply again with few switchbacks through aspen stands and boulder fields.

The climb to Half Moon Pass is long and steady, hugging tree line along the way. There is much rejoicing when we crest the pass and start walking downhill, this time to the end. The grade is gradual and passes through a rainbow of wildflower meadows among green mosses, grasses, and shrubs. This final, long descent takes us back, at long last, to the trailhead.

34 | FOUR SCORE

Round trip	■	**7 miles**
Loop direction	■	Clockwise
Hiking time	■	4 to 5 hours
Sweat factor	■	High+
Starting elevation	■	12,000 feet
High point	■	14,286 feet
Low point	■	12,000 feet
Elevation gain	■	3422 feet
Best hiking season	■	Early July through October
Maps	■	USGS Alma
Contact	■	Pike National Forest

Driving directions: To get here, follow Colorado 9 15 miles south of Breckenridge to Alma. Look for a little Kite Lake sign on the west side of the road, hang a right, and follow the scenic gravel road up Buckskin Gulch to its end at the Kite Lake trailhead and campground. Expect big crowds on weekends, and start early to miss afternoon storms.

Bagging fourteeners is a popular activity in Colorado, and this place gets you three in one day, plus a bonus peak. A hugely popular day-hike destination, these four mountains bordering the Continental Divide between Breckenridge and Fairplay offer hikers the opportunity to take on the challenge of multiple high peaks on one route, or choose one or two of your favorites. Relatively shallow saddles make for "easy" access between the summits, but it is a challenging day all the same. Make no mistake, climbing any mountain at this altitude is not for the faint of heart; prepare wisely for maximum fun. Each peak has its own personality, and all have outstanding views.

Note: We wavered on our decision to include this hike for the very reason stated above: chalking up fourteener peaks is so popular that our favorite mountains are being loved to death. With such easy access to this hike, these mountains are taking the hit especially hard. Please, tread as softly as you can, don't leave trash behind, and love the place lightly.

The trail begins at the south end of Kite Lake on a well-trodden trail past the campground, which is mostly a Woodstock-like collection of tents set up hither and yon near the lake. Follow the path past the lake toward a huge bowl and begin the steep initial climb on loose rock. We have gained a couple of hundred feet already, standing now on

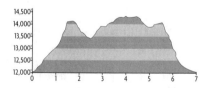

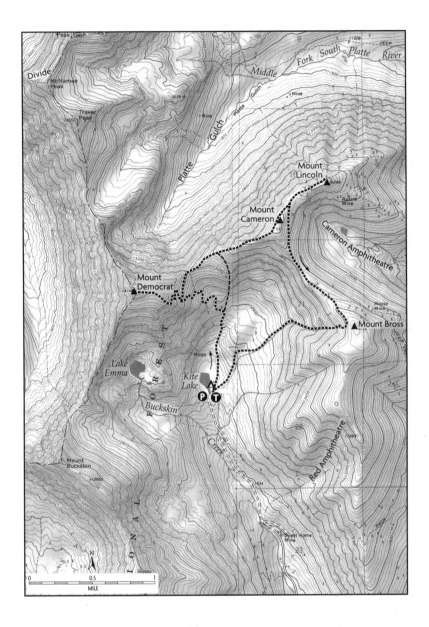

a shelf of this bowl. Check out the sweet views of the gulch and Mount Buckskin behind us. Relics of this area's molybdenum mining days are scattered about these lower slopes as we continue up a massive talus field to a junction. A left turn here is the most direct route to Mount Democrat, but continue heading straight up to the saddle, then turn uphill. We'll take the express route, following a breadcrumb trail of cairns up a steep, rocky slope. Switchbacks ease the burden a bit, but we are gaining elevation and losing oxygen in a hurry. The views are already amazing—Buckskin Gulch unfolds down the valley, Mount Bross looms from the east, and Mount Cameron waits for our arrival. There is a false summit ahead and on top are out-of-this-world views to the north of Platte Gulch and the rugged peaks of the Continental Divide, dominated by 14,265-foot Quandary Peak. Take a look over your shoulder at the skinny and steep ridge climbing to Cameron. That's phase two of this hike. Keep climbing up a final slope of boulders, then one more steep grunt to the summit of Mount Democrat at 14,148 feet. As expected, there are beauteous views of mountains everywhere, like the Mosquito Range to the south, north to the Gore and Tenmile Ranges, and the wide open land of South Park to the east. We also have an aerial view of the Climax Mine way below.

Time to move on to mountain number two. We'll descend the same way, using caution on the rocks, and follow a faint trail that slants to the saddle

Mount Lincoln on approach from Cameron

below. There is a gnarly view of Quandary Peak straight north, and an aged mine shaft next to the trail. After a short scramble over a rocky section, there is a respectable trail following this steep, narrow ridge. The views north are distractingly gorgeous, and Mount Bross flaunts its ample girth, too, vying for our attention. Back the other way is a nice look at Mount Democrat's pointy peak, and the aptly titled Kite Lake far below. The trail gets fairly easy toward the top, and before we know it we are strolling across the spacious summit of Mount Cameron at 14,239 feet. Technically speaking, Cameron is not a "real" fourteener since its elevation is less than 150 feet below that of Mount Lincoln next door. And since these two peaks are joined by a saddle, poor old Cameron has been relegated as just a shoulder of Lincoln—kind of like a little sidecar attached to a big Harley, or like Tonto and the Lone Ranger. The big guy gets all the glory. It is widely accepted that Cameron is not an official fourteener, and most guidebooks and barstool banter will whistle the same tune. However, it stands over 14,000 feet, it felt like 14,000 coming up, and in this book Mount Cameron joins the big boys.

That said, we can enjoy an easy trek across this moonscape of a summit down to a long, sweeping saddle and start another grind up to Mount Lincoln. The skinny path rises along the northwest curve of the peak to a craggy collection of rock slabs and rust-colored boulders, and a final kick takes us to the 14,286-foot high point of Mount Lincoln. This is a fun fourteener, a tight fist of rugged rock standing tall among exceptional views in every direction, like Mount of the Holy Cross way over there to the west, and Mounts Massive and Elbert in the southwest. Pretty cool, eh?

Below Lincoln's south face is the Cameron Amphitheatre, a huge bowl littered with mine tailings and shafts burrowed into the hill. Mount Bross is on the other side; one more climb on this ambitious hike. To get over there, we'll just scramble back down the rocks to the saddle, follow the clear path on a long ridgeline below Mount Cameron, and head uphill again. The trail here is a wide access "road" from mining days, and while nontechnical and easy to negotiate, the grade is steep enough to make it a challenge after climbing three peaks prior. Keep slogging ahead across this featureless mound to a large cairn wind shelter at 14,172 feet. There is plenty of room on top of Bross—if someone brought a football, break it out and let's get a game going.

Descending back to Kite Lake is a long ordeal, but there are several choices of routes to fit your current state of exhaustion. Some trails make long traverses across the hillside; others just shoot right down one of two drainages to the bottom. Today, we'll take the faster way, skipping long strides on a deep layer of tailings in a narrow fold in the west wall of Bross. The drainage spills into a ridge layered with green grass and wildflowers of blue, purple, and pink, and little streamlets trickling among hummocks of spongy earth. The path descends one final slope and skirts the lake to the trailhead, thus ending another splendid day in the mountains.

35 PTARMIGAN TRAIL

Round trip ■	7 miles
Loop direction ■	Clockwise
Hiking time ■	5 hours
Sweat factor ■	Low+ to moderate
Starting elevation ■	9095 feet
High point ■	11,483 feet
Low point ■	9095 feet
Elevation gain ■	2605 feet
Best hiking season ■	June through October
Maps ■	USGS Dillon
Contact ■	Arapaho National Forest

Driving directions: Access to this trail is easy; just exit Interstate 70 at Dillon/Silverthorne and head north on Colorado 9 a few hundred yards to Tanglewood Lane. Follow this road around to a right turn onto Ptarmigan Trail Road (County Road 2021). The trailhead and a small parking turnout are on top of the hill.

Here is an excellent lollipop loop in the hills above Silverthorne in a small triangle of the Williams Fork Mountains and Arapaho National Forest. The route is a mellow stroll on a gentle grade and soft tread through aspen and pine forest, with great views of the Gore Range, Dillon Reservoir, and the high mountains far to the south.

This hike kicks off with a short climb through a little stand of trees and up a steep gravel road to the top of the hill, where the trail continues up a dry, south-facing slope of stubby sage and grasses. As we pass under a huge power pole, note the faint trail coming in from the right; that is our return route. Just past this junction, the path leads into a forest mix of pine and aspen. The trail is in superb condition, hugging the contours of the mountain on soft tread and easy, even flat grades in these early stages. Breaks in the trees here and there expose great views of Buffalo Mountain, Dillon Reservoir, and the Gore Range. This is a fantastic autumn hike, and on a day like today we are rewarded with a shimmering veil of golden light in these gorgeous aspen forests. We'll hop over a few skinny creeks trickling down the folds of the hills to an easy uphill stretch that brings us to an overlook on an outcrop of rock at around the 2-mile mark, with fine views of Silverthorne below and the Gore Range and Eagles Nest Wilderness beyond. Past the overlook, the grade finally gets a

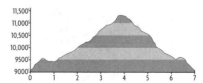

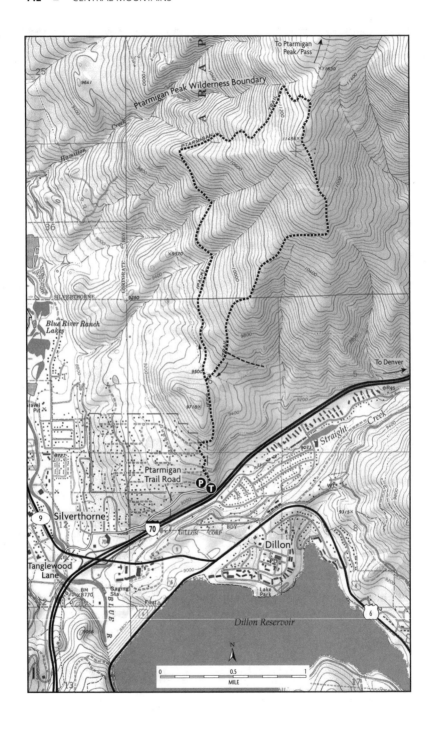

Ptarmigan Trail

bit steeper, and soon the trees slowly disperse and we are at the Ptarmigan Peak Wilderness Boundary. The wide-open tundra ahead is part of the giant mountain that makes up Ptarmigan Peak, way off in the northeast distance. The trail to the peak continues from here for a nice multiday trek. From this junction, we will split off onto the trail just before the boundary sign, descending gently into the woods. Well, it starts out gently, but the path soon sheds elevation fast and steeply, with no switchbacks to ease the burn in our quads. In fact, there is virtually nothing to slow us down except a host of big piles of gravel posing as water bars. It's a tough descent on the legs, but it gets down in a hurry. Before we know it, another junction appears at the bottom of this hill, and a right turn takes us back to the powerline and the stem of the trail. A left here leads back to the trailhead and the knowledge that good eats are available in town.

36 CRATER LAKE TRAIL

Round trip ■	**4 miles**
Loop direction ■	Counterclockwise
Hiking time ■	2 hours
Sweat factor ■	Low+
Starting elevation ■	9560 feet
High point ■	10,171 feet
Low point ■	9560 feet
Elevation gain ■	698 feet
Best hiking season ■	June through October
Maps ■	USGS Maroon Bells; National Forest Service, White River
Contact ■	White River National Forest, Aspen District

Driving directions: To get here from Aspen, take Colorado 82 north out of town to West Maroon Creek Road and hang a left. Follow this road to the Forest Service entrance station, fork over the $10 daily fee, and continue on the road 5 miles to the day use parking area at Maroon Lake.

Note: In summer months, shuttle buses transport visitors to Maroon Lake every 20 minutes from the Aspen Highlands Village base area. The fare is $5 round trip for adults and comes with an entertaining narrative. The road is closed from 9 AM to 5 PM to all vehicles at this time except for the buses, so get here early or plan for extra travel time. Call the Roaring Fork Transit Agency at (970) 925-8484 or the Aspen Ranger Station at (970) 925-3445 for the latest info.

This is one of the shorter hikes in the book, but the setting is so exquisite it is difficult to even begin walking. The view right at the trailhead is one of the most unforgettable in Colorado. After a short stroll past Maroon Lake, we'll take off on a trail through aspen and spruce to Crater Lake for an up-close experience of the stunning Maroon Bells. Come here in the fall when the aspen and the Bells try to outdo each other's beauty. It is an absolutely fabulous hike and an all-time author favorite.

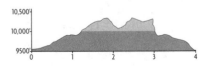

Forgive us if we are rendered speechless, standing here staring up at these impossibly beautiful mountains. The view out there is so perfect we could turn around and leave right now and feel content that we saw something special. Surely this must be the high court of all things alpine, and we have been brought before the throne of their kings. The Maroon Bells, resplendent in dress whites of virgin snow, stand stalwart against the western sky—and believe us, they carry high their mantle of Colorado's wilderness image. With springs in our steps on this clear, fresh autumn day, we march right into paradise.

Skirting Maroon Lake on the trail of the same name, we merge with the Crater Lake Trail at the Deadly Bells kiosk. There is fascinating information here on the mountains ahead and stern reminders of how dangerous and unpredictable they are, should you choose to climb high into their clutches. The official loop portion of this hike is over there to the left, down the Scenic Loop Trail, which we will sample on the return leg. Shortly past the split, we enter the famed Maroon Bells-Snowmass Wilderness, and gradually climb above and away from the lake and upper riparian areas into a majestic stand of aspen. The grade gets somewhat steeper through more woods of pine and aspen, and we have great views of the equally impressive 14,018-foot Pyramid Peak to our left. The path scrambles over a large field of huge boulders and talus scattered all over, and all the while we see one spectacular view of the Bells after another. And that was just the prelude to the showcase

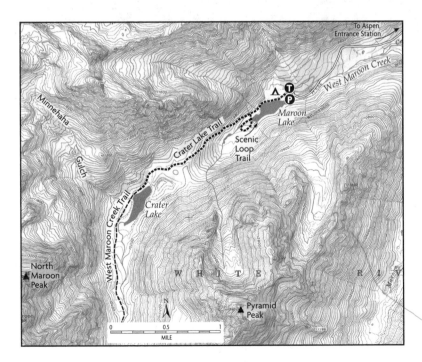

The Maroon Bells

scene up ahead. Lean left at the West Maroon Creek Trail (a right here heads up to Buckskin Pass); a few dozen steps later we are at the shores of Crater Lake. This is why we love the high country so much. The lake is absolutely still and silent, a liquid mirror reflecting the majesty of North and South Maroon Peaks. The image in the water is so clear and complete that it is difficult to tell which view is real. The cuts in the rock that appeared as thin lines from the trailhead have come to life as giant serrations on the nearly vertical faces of the peaks. The summits are sharp, daunting spikes that seem unattainable. What a glorious place. Nature has dealt a generous hand with the Maroon Bells.

The struggle to get up and leave here is great, but sooner or later the sun will go down, so let's head back. The views going this direction are plenty nice, as well. The U-shaped valley is full of aspen, and they are alight in golden dress, flanked by steep ridges crowned in ragged promontories of reddish rock. We'll retrace our steps back down the trail to the junction with the Scenic Loop Trail and a right turn on the path along the west edge of Maroon Lake. Just before the bridge, turn right again on the trail following Maroon Creek and its verdant riparian landscape. We'll skip the second bridge upstream and follow the sign for the Upper Scenic Loop, climbing gently into a gorgeous aspen stand on a skinny path with pint-size boulders and roots. This is another place to stop and listen—to the creek whispering by our feet and to the aspen leaves tick-ticking in the wind, sprinkling sunshine all over the place.

Around the next bend, the trail turns back toward the valley, rolling up and down some small hillocks back to the bridge crossing the creek, which we will cross and head back up to Maroon Lake Trail for the return along Maroon Lake to the trailhead.

37 ┆ EAGLESMERE LOOP

Round trip ■	**9.3 miles**
Loop direction ■	Counterclockwise
Hiking time ■	6 hours
Sweat factor ■	Moderate++
Starting elevation ■	8720 feet
High point ■	10,400 feet
Low point ■	8600 feet
Elevation gain ■	1800 feet
Best hiking season ■	June through October
Maps ■	USGS Mount Powell
Contact ■	Arapaho National Forest, Dillon Ranger District

Driving directions: To get here from Silverthorne, follow Colorado 9 north from Interstate 70 for 17 miles and turn left onto Heeney Road 30, at the south end of Green Mountain Reservoir. Follow this road 5.5 miles to the junction with Forest Road 1725. Follow Forest Road 1725 for 2 miles and veer right at a fork to Forest Road 1726 to reach the upper parking lot and the Eaglesmere trailhead.

This one has it all. Damp, dark underbellies of lush pine forests, open, soft expanses of aspen groves, and unobstructed views of some of Colorado's gnarliest peaks, all nestled in the Eagles Nest Wilderness north of the Gore Range. Even better, this area is full of hidden treasures cached amidst a range of mostly unnamed peaks.

Heading west from the trailhead, the trail is immediately immersed in a thick stand of aspen. After flirting with expansive views through the trees, we pop out onto a ridge with a gorgeous look at Gore Range and Lower Cataract Lake and its attendant waterfall. The trail heads

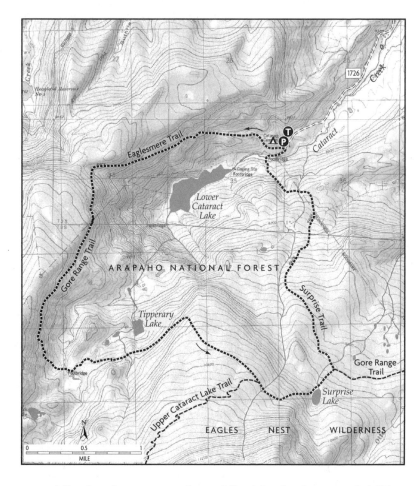

west, following the contours of a rapidly rising landscape and drifting through postcard scenery. A short way ahead, a smudge of Green Mountain Reservoir moves into view to the east, along with the western ridges of the Williams Fork Mountains. Approaching 2 miles, the trail turns south and continues to climb. The landscape changes drastically here as we enter a primeval setting of lichen-covered lodgepole pine and aspen pockets in shallow valleys.

Crossing the boundary into the Eagle Nest Wilderness, the trail begins a steep traverse up a hillside heading south. Just shy of 3 miles, the Eaglesmere Trail meets the Gore Range Trail. A right leads up to Eaglesmere Lakes and beyond; we'll turn left onto the Gore Range Trail and continue hiking south. Past the junction, our lungs get a respite as the trail descends through the soft greens of these woods. The trail twists around a couple of switchbacks as it winds down over loose rocks, exposed roots, and a lot of fallen logs. As the trail begins to wrap eastward, we will move through quietly flowing creeks and streams scribbled on a landscape of large granite boulders and ponds. Follow the bridges and a number of cairns east past Cataract Creek to the junction with Tipperary Lake at around 4 miles. There is a great view and a fine place for a break down the short, steep path to the lake. After a rest, we'll continue heading east on the Gore Range Trail, steadily gaining elevation with few spots of reprieve. Aside from offering an occasional glimpse of the Gore Range through the trees, this soft dirt trail pierces a shut-in world of thousands of fallen trees draped in moss. The junction with the Upper Cataract Lake Trail comes along at the 5-mile mark, and we will trudge right on by, crossing the drainage past the trail sign. This is the high point of the trail; the rest of the hike is mostly downhill.

After a short descent eastward, Surprise Lake comes out of nowhere. The path crosses the drainage exiting the north end of the lake and continues to the last junction of the trip. We leave the Gore Range Trail here and turn left onto Surprise Trail in the final northerly push back to the trailhead. This last

Quiet rest stop on Eaglesmere Loop

part of the hike heads north and descends a steep grade with loose rocks, fallen trees, and renegade roots. The trail winds down the hill, paralleling a creek to our left, and aspen begin to reemerge amidst the pine. Our route curls through some open glades back to the west across a few more streams, then heads over one last wooden bridge to the Surprise trailhead. Turn right and walk east down the short road to the junction to the parking area, and go left up the last stretch to the Eaglesmere trailhead.

SOUTHWEST MOUNTAINS

38 | FOURMILE FALLS

Round trip	**11 miles**
Loop direction	Counterclockwise
Hiking time	6 hours
Sweat factor	High
Starting elevation	9062 feet
High point	11,225 feet
Low point	9019 feet
Elevation gain	2850 feet
Best hiking season	June through October
Maps	USGS Pagosa Springs
Contact	San Juan National Forest

Driving directions: To get here from the heart of Pagosa Springs, follow Fourmile Road due north from US 160 13 miles to the road's end at a parking area and the trailhead.

We sort of stumbled upon this trail, and it turned out to be another favorite. How can you beat a long day hike in the exquisite Weminuche Wilderness? The hike is loaded with stunning scenery, more than a dozen waterfalls—one of them the 300-foot Fourmile Falls—and a dreamy high mountain lake. The trail condition is excellent nearly the entire trip, with a couple of stream crossings and fine views of neighboring mountains.

Starting at 9000 feet and change, we already have glimpses of a few of the high mountains of the beauteous Weminuche, like Quien Sabe and Eagle Peaks. The trail travels soft tread in a forest of monster aspen and Engelmann spruce. The path descends gradually to Fourmile Creek, then up a small hill on the other side. After only about 0.5 mile we arrive at the Weminuche Wilderness boundary, with spectacular views to the north. Follow the trail down the steep, rocky section to a scenic little valley near the creek dotted with groves of spruce. Ahead is a long, open meadow on generally level ground, then back to a mix of pine and aspen. The

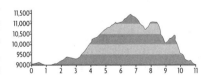

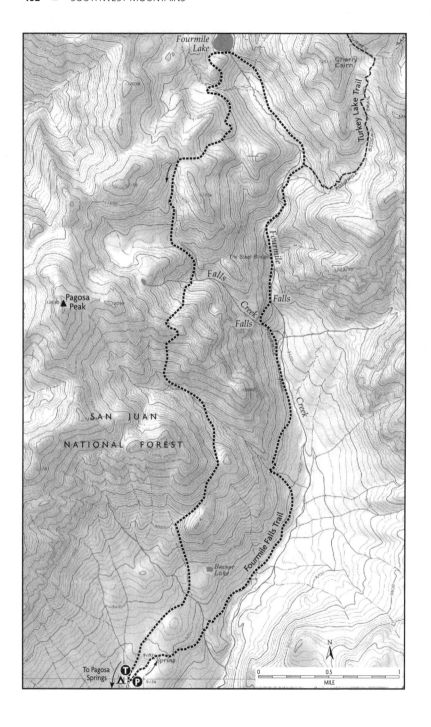

trail begins to climb and crosses a tributary creek of Fourmile, followed by a stroll among giant spruce and fir. A big elevation gain is coming soon, but for now we enjoy gentle undulations in the hill. Before long, we break free of the trees for our first glimpse of the lofty Fourmile Falls at just over 3 miles—long tendrils of water freefall 300 feet over the face of the rock, with another tier closer to the bottom. The water plummets into a huge amphitheatre bowl with a small pool of Falls Creek. We'll cross the creek, make a long, rocky climb on the other side, and segue back into scenic woods. With the image of the big falls still fresh in our minds, we come to another huge waterfall, a thundering, agitated number on Fourmile Creek, this time walking at the head of the falls and looking down. Cross here (this makes four stream crossings so far, with a lot more to come) and follow close to the creek along the base of a high ridge on a long, steady ascent on rocky tread to another waterfall. It looks like just another traverse of the creek, but this time we're almost sure to get wet. Once upon a time, there was a sturdy steel bridge here, but at the time of this writing it's long gone. The current is strong, the water is cold, and there is no easy crossing on boulders or logs—time to go wading. To the left is another huge waterfall, a slender, attractive beauty cascading down a tall cliff and providing a compelling distraction from ice-cold toes.

Past the falls, the trail climbs over a ridge, then drops back down again for another jump over the creek, easier this time with rocks for steps. Yet another gorgeous waterfall, about 50 frothy feet high, appears in a skinny gorge. Great views of 12,500-foot Cherry Cairn are in our sights, and a short way farther is another tricky stream crossing, then a steady, steeper ascent through the woods, past another falls. At about the 5-mile mark is the junction with the Turkey Lake Trail; our path to Fourmile Lake keeps on straight ahead. Climb past another small waterfall and up a gentle, barely noticeable ascent through a quiet, open meadow of tall grasses and scattered pine stands. Following the creek's banks along easy bends, the path heads back into the woods, climbs a bit steeper past a couple more falls, then reaches the storybook setting of Fourmile Lake. This is the headwaters of the creek and all those waterfalls—beautiful, green-tinted waters with big rainbow trout, giant mountains on three sides, and a fringe of deep-green pine forest. The place was made to order for a rest stop and a nap. Time to sit back and linger a bit.

Continuing the trek, we'll follow the trail into the woods to a sign for the Anderson Trail, angle slightly southeast up a short climb, then mosey through the trees to another scenic creek and a large open wetland area. It is more shaded and cooler on this side, hence the snow beneath our boots. The path turns a few times and begins descending, with a nice view of Pagosa Peak through the trees. The trail is not in the best condition over here, with deep erosion gullies, a lot of muddy sections, and water flowing right down the path. Use caution and tread as lightly as you can. Soon the trail switchbacks down and we're treated to amazing views of all 12,640 feet of Pagosa Peak.

Up ahead is a pretty meadow and a big amphitheater bowl of the peak skirts the base of the mountain. Past the meadow, we descend in earnest down switchbacks with beautiful, far-off views of the Wolf Creek Pass area, and of the San Juan Mountains and the Continental Divide in the distance. A stunning aspen stand is a final treat closer to the bottom. In the fall, it feels alive with good cheer and lifts tired spirits after the long slog prior. We'll alternate through pine and aspen here on this fun final stretch to the trailhead, concluding the day at just shy of six hours.

Fourmile Falls

39 PETROGLYPH POINT TRAIL

Round trip	■	**2.8 miles**
Loop direction	■	Counterclockwise
Hiking time	■	2 hours
Sweat factor	■	Easy
Starting elevation	■	6900 feet
High point	■	6930 feet
Low point	■	6650 feet
Elevation gain	■	554 feet
Best hiking season	■	Year-round, but best from April through June, and late fall
Maps	■	USGS Point Lookout
Contact	■	Mesa Verde National Park

Driving directions: To reach the park, drive west from Durango on US 160. Turn south at the Mesa Verde National Park turnoff, pay the required fees and pick up a map at the park entrance station, then follow the signs to the Spruce Tree House parking lot. The trail begins just south of the Chapin Mesa Museum.

This trail offers an opportunity for a close-up view of Mesa Verde National Park. Depending on the heat, it is an easy hike that accommodates most walkers eager to delve a bit deeper into this popular park. The hike is short, but offers something car-bound visitors miss: an easy trek that follows the curvy rim of a deep canyon speckled with rolling waves of juniper and piñon. It's a self-guided interpretive trail that educates as much as it astounds. The largest set of petroglyphs in the park greets the sun-soaked hiker at the far end of the loop, along with a story of the Anasazi carved into the side of a cliff more than one thousand years ago! Be sure to bring plenty of water for this one, as the sun blasts the area. Wear sunscreen, too, lest you resemble a lobster at the end of the day.

Be sure to allow time to check out the ruin and museum before or after the hike. A self-guided tour to the well-preserved Spruce Tree House is a must-do side trip. Certain other ruins here require tickets, which can be purchased at the visitor center; however, the Spruce Tree House is free.

Let's start the hike by following the paved trail behind the museum winding down toward the cliff dwelling. Look for signs indicating the official beginning of the Petroglyph Point Trail at 0.1 mile. Registration is required at either the museum or the trailhead. The registry at the trailhead also has trail guides, which can be purchased for fifty cents. Four bits well spent,

these guides give detailed information concerning the park's flora, fauna, geology, and even a key to decipher the petroglyphs on the loop.

The paved path gives way to a soft dirt trail as it begins to head south out onto the mesa. At 0.2 mile, we'll turn left up the rock steps toward

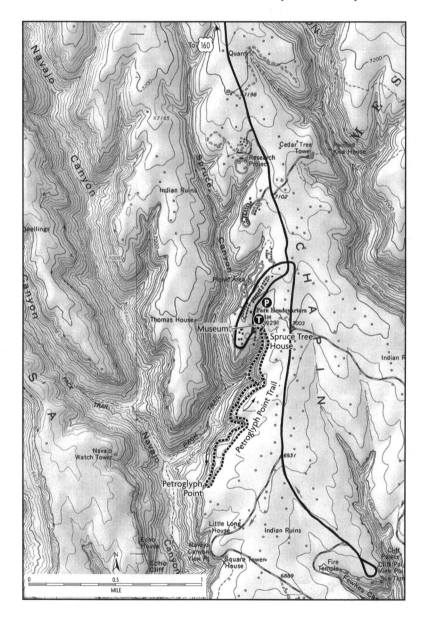

Petroglyphs at Mesa Verde (Photo by Sierra Overlie)

Petroglyph Point. The trail begins to wind south on the side of a west-facing rim affording great views of Spruce Canyon and Long Mesa beyond. Tracing the wrinkles of the canyon, our route wanders in and out of enormous rock shelves, up and down rock steps, and past amazing shapes grooved into the sandstone by an inland ocean eons ago. At 1.35 miles, out near the far end of the loop, the trail passes the petroglyphs for which it is named. Linger here a bit and imagine the Anasazi sculpting these designs into the rock one thousand years ago. Check the back of the trail guide for a Hopi interpretation of the glyphs. Some of the symbols denote different clans, including the

Eagle, Mountain Sheep, and Parrot. Others declare "The place where the Pueblo People emerged from the earth." Still others describe this as where the migration of these peoples ended.

Just past the petroglyphs, the trail climbs another series of rock steps, which pass a nice overlook of the confluence of Navajo and Spruce Canyons before topping out on the rim of the canyon that had to this point towered above. Now we head back north, following the return trail that essentially parallels the outgoing trail, only now on top of the mesa. After passing through a pygmy forest, the trail enters a world of barren trees, the result of a fire that swept through Mesa Verde in 2003. At 2.5 miles, the trail begins to cross over the top of the shelf that encloses the Spruce Tree House. A left turn just past the dwelling leads back to the Chapin Mesa Museum and the conclusion of this short loop back in time.

40 STORMS GULCH TRAIL

Round trip ■	**5.75 miles**
Loop direction ■	Counterclockwise
Hiking time ■	3 hours
Sweat factor ■	Moderate
Starting elevation ■	8460 feet
High point ■	10,534 feet
Low point ■	8389 feet
Elevation gain ■	2306 feet
Best hiking season ■	June through October
Maps ■	USGS Ouray; Ouray Trails Group, *Hiking Trails of Ouray County*
Contact ■	Uncompahgre National Forest

Driving directions: To get here from Ouray, take Colorado 550 north out of town to County Road 14. This road curves through a residential area and climbs to the split with County Road 14A. A left turn here leads 2.5 miles to a dead end and a small parking area. The trail starts here.

Welcome to the Switzerland of America! Surrounded by arguably the most beautiful mountains in Colorado, Ouray is a premier year-round destination for outdoor enthusiasts. The town came to life in 1875 with the discovery of gold and silver, and remained vibrant with visitors traveling to enjoy the area's majestic scenery. The mountains in this part of the state never fail to deliver: high, rugged peaks rise in every direction, with even the little ones boasting upward of 11,000 feet, and hundreds of clear, cold streams flow through narrow gorges and wide valleys. Ouray is full of enchanting

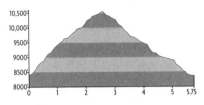

Victorian homes, and Main Street boasts classic buildings like the St. Elmo Hotel, Beaumont Hotel, and Livery Barn. There are more than forty superb hiking trails in Ouray County to complement the town's charm, and this one lives up to expectations with excellent trail conditions, challenging terrain, and unbelievable views.

Note: The Ouray Mountain Rescue Team reminds us that trails in this area are located in rugged wilderness or otherwise remote regions. Help could be a long time coming. Terrain is demanding, and even experienced hikers have been lost. Hiking at high altitudes is a hard, tiring, thirsty challenge, and mountain distances can be deceptive. Use your head and be smart when choosing a route.

Follow the gnarly four-wheel-drive road down the steep, rocky hill, cross Cutler Creek, and climb the other side 0.7 mile to the official trailhead. A sign is posted for the Baldy Trail to the left (we will return from that way); our route today goes right on the Storms Gulch Trail, into a beautiful aspen stand on a narrow and rugged path. We wisely chose the best time of the year, as the fall colors dress the land in its Sunday best. A friendly little creek joins us for a short way as the trail gently undulates through mountain mahogany and aspen to the junction with the Shortcut Trail and the boundary of the Uncompahgre Wilderness. We will lean left here, staying on the Storms Gulch Trail just inside the boundary. The trail climbs steeply for a while through an arid landscape of sage, Gambel oak, and ponderosa pine. A bend to the left turns our attention to the splendiferous view of the range of mountains to the south. High, snow-dusted peaks are trimmed with thick pine forest and meadows of green foliage. What a sight.

The trail continues to climb steeply, generally following the natural contours of this side of the gulch. Up there to our left is the high ridgeline we are shooting for, and Baldy Peak is just beyond. This is an excellent trail with a primitive feel, and we have the place all to ourselves. Not only that, there are several options to connect to a string of other loop trails penetrating deeper into the wilderness. Up a couple more switchbacks, we arrive at an exposed ridge above the gulch. Here, the path angles northwest into a grove of aspen, up a steep grade, and then downhill into more aspen. It is an easy stroll here on almost level ground, with an occasional hiccup in the terrain followed by one more moderate climb to reach the junction with the Baldy Trail and Baldy Peak Trail. We'll go left, in the direction of the peak, delving briefly into a thick grove of spruce then past another aspen stand. The trees here have more elbow room and are gnarly and height-challenged due to the exposure to intense weather. The trail parallels these durable aspen to one last uphill grind to the top of the ridge. There is an incredible view east of Courthouse Mountain and more beauteous peaks in the Uncompahgre Wilderness. Stay the course

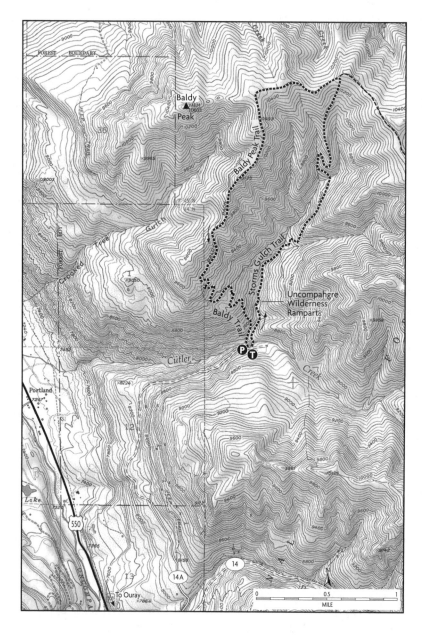

through these pines (there is usually a well-trod horse trail leading the way) to an open ridge and a breathtaking mountain scene. Look east at giant mountains like Uncompahgre Peak and Wetterhorn Peak, both fourteeners, and

Matterhorn Peak, a high thirteener. The valley we just hiked looks even more beautiful from up here, painted in assorted shades of green, which in turn are mottled with gold. Look west at the postcard-perfect Sneffels Range, with Mount Sneffels itself standing proud among its brethren. If you're interested in a short side trip, the trail accessing Baldy Peak heads over there from here. By the way, on a clear day like this, look to the western horizon, way, way out there. Those are the La Sal Mountains in Utah. This is one of those hikes where you walk along with a big ol' grin on your face the whole time, mighty glad to be in such a glorious place.

From here, the trail follows this ridgeline down into the trees, making one sweep through a shallow glade of aspen. Stop for a minute beneath the mantle of gold, take a deep breath, and feel the very spirit of autumn, borne on whispers of wind. A long series of switchbacks leads down the home-stretch to the trailhead. The grade is only moderate here, and the descent is rather enjoyable. Up ahead is a large grove of Gambel oak, forming a tunnel of gnarled, leafy appendages all the way to one last fringe of aspen, then the junction with the gulch trail. A right turn down the stem of the loop takes us back to the trailhead.

Postcard mountains above Ouray

41 JUD WIEBE TRAIL

Round trip ■	**3.3 miles**
Loop direction ■	Counterclockwise
Hiking time ■	2.5 hours
Sweat factor ■	Moderate
Starting elevation ■	8838 feet
High point ■	9889 feet
Low point ■	8838 feet
Elevation gain ■	1517 feet
Best hiking season ■	May through October
Maps ■	USGS Telluride
Contact ■	Uncompahgre National Forest

Driving directions: To reach the trailhead, follow US 550 to Colorado 62, and head west to Colorado 145. Follow Colorado 145 east into Telluride to North Oak Street. Turn left here to the junction with Tomboy Road. The hike starts here.

It is difficult to find many areas around Telluride that are not breathtaking and the Jud Wiebe Trail is certainly no exception. This quaint village sits in the valley of some of the most beautiful mountain scenery in Colorado, and is a perfect place to rendezvous for some great hiking. Settled as a gold-mining town in the late 1800s, Telluride quickly gained notoriety as a rowdy town with a boisterous population, like Butch Cassidy and other hooligans. Its reputation was so sketchy that train conductors would announce "to-hell-you-ride" when they arrived, and local legend has it that the town was named after this foreboding welcome. This hike, however, boasts just how gorgeous Telluride is by swiftly climbing above the town for soaring views of the area, and just as abruptly travels clear of civilization into rugged wilderness in the direction of the upper reaches of the massive Sneffels Range. A peaceful ascent near the end of the hike reveals dynamite looks at this area's signature eastern mountains and the breathtaking 365-foot Bridal Veil Falls.

The trail begins by climbing the rugged Tomboy Road eastward, which rises above Telluride straight away and serves up great views of the colorful town below. Only a short way up the road, we will exit at a left turn onto the Jud Wiebe Trail. Thus begins a stiff ascent up this south-facing slope, bending around switchbacks into the aspen-covered hillside. Directly south, the Bear

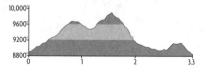

Creek Basin, with Ballard Mountain in the foreground, steadily unfolds as the trail climbs northwest. Just short of 1 mile, the trail splits toward one of a few social trails. These trails

will lead you straight up against the grain of the mountainside for a strenuous and erosion-promoting climb. Don't go that way. Stay on the main path and follow the switchbacks to help preserve its integrity. Eventually the zigzags end and the trail continues on a more gradual grade northwest through a mixture of spruce and aspen.

The trail plateaus and begins a short descent to the next junction at 1.3 miles, where we will keep right on shuffling along the Jud Wiebe Trail. Winding through a soft landscape thick with spruce and fir trees, look for glimpses north of the extensive San Juan Range. The second steady climb of the day introduces itself just after crossing Cornet Creek, adapting to the contours of the mountain as it slices up through a south-facing hillside swollen with aspen. Just over a half-mile past the creek, our path tops out onto an open stretch and the best views of the hike. Look east toward Telluride and Ajax Peaks, the signature mountains creating the spectacular Bridal Veil Falls. We'll leave the plateau and drop west back into the trees, accented by an assortment of wildflowers as the trail continues west. At 2.3 miles, there is a junction with the Mill Creek and Deep Creek trails, providing access to the Sneffels Highline Trail. Let's head straight on the Jud Wiebe Trail.

The last junction is at 2.7 miles. Here, we have a choice of turning right to finish the loop, or left toward Cornet Falls. Take our advice and make the 0.4-mile journey up this beautiful sandstone canyon to the high, narrow falls.

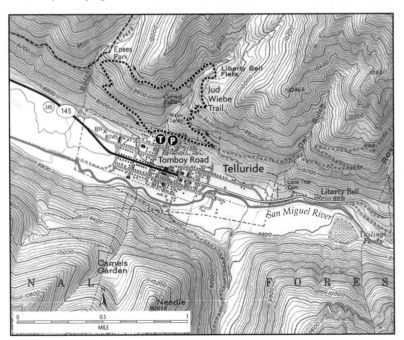

Hiking the Jud Wiebe Trail

It is a beautiful sight, indeed, and a perfect conclusion to this great hike. After loitering at the falls a bit, we'll follow the trail to North Aspen Street, turn left on West Galena Avenue, and then take one more left onto North Oak Street to the trailhead.

42 WILSON MESA LOOP

Round trip ■	5.5 miles
Loop direction ■	Clockwise
Hiking time ■	2.5 hours
Sweat factor ■	Moderate
Starting elevation ■	9753 feet
High point ■	10,155 feet
Low point ■	9224 feet
Elevation gain ■	1415 feet
Best hiking season ■	May through September
Maps ■	USGS Telluride
Contact ■	Uncompahgre National Forest

Driving directions: The trailhead lies at the end of a series of forest roads. Follow Colorado 145 west from Telluride to Ilium Road (Forest

Road 625). Head south 2.3 miles to the intersection with 63J Road, also known as Forest Road 623 or Sunshine Mesa Road, and turn right. Follow 63J for 5.5 miles, past Galloping Goose Trail to the

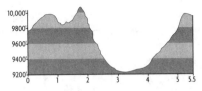

Wilson Mesa Trail at the end of the road. The road becomes difficult for low-clearance cars toward the end, but remains passable.

With the grandeur of Wilson Peak, rushing rivers and waterfalls, and a carnival of diverse wildflowers, this trail provides a wonderfully colorful day trip. Just southwest of Telluride, this is yet another breathtaking hike to add to the area's repertoire already rife with outdoor treasures. Wilson Peak looms close by, and dazzling waterfalls and gushing creeks soothe our senses for much of the way. The hike takes us through pine and aspen forests, past Wilson Peak, over a pleasant creek to the remains of an old mine and its shaft and railway, before winding through absurdly beautiful meadows of flowers.

This lollipop loop starts right out with a short climb to the south before shifting west. As it steadily gains elevation, the wide dirt trail leads through a nice mixture of tall aspen and pine. Stay alert through this section, as it is also shared with mountain bikes and motorcycles. At 0.6 mile, a junction indicates the beginning of the actual loop. Let's go clockwise today, staying straight and west on the Sunshine Mesa Trail through an amazing abundance of wildflowers. As the trail wraps south, slicing through a steep west-facing slope, the awesome sight of 14,017-foot Wilson Peak is an ample distraction from the extensive variety of flora. We will hike on soft dirt and talus and over an occasional drainage as the path winds up the valley separating Wilson Peak on our right and Sunshine Mountain on our left. Hike slower through this stretch of the trail—huge rock formations buttress the trail, splashing waterfalls on both sides feed Bilk Creek, the mountains enclosing Telluride loom to the north, and the wildflowers appear to be endless.

Approaching 2 miles, the trail descends and crosses Bilk Creek before meeting the junction with Lizard Head Trail. Look for the gnarled remnants of a mining railway leading into an abandoned shaft. A common sight on many trails surrounding Telluride, the old and mangled remains of twisted metal provide a poignant reminder of the area's mining history. Immediately after crossing the creek, look for a partially hidden sign indicating the northward course of the Lizard Head Trail. After this sharp right turn, the trail begins a descent on the west side of Bilk Creek. We'll cruise down the open valley, steeply at times, enjoying great views north toward the Sneffels Range and east toward Sunshine Mountain. After a couple of switchbacks, the Lizard Head Trail bottoms out next to the creek at 2.7 miles, providing a great area to shed our packs for a short rest.

For the next mile, the trail winds in and out of open valleys and shaded dells in its northern pursuit to the next junction with the Wilson Mesa Trail. This is a right turn for us, heading east back toward the Sunshine Mesa Trail, ascending steeply into a dense grove of aspen. Wilson Peak returns to view as the trail switchbacks southeast, passing a small pond and continuing to gain elevation, now heading directly south toward the end of the loop. At 4.9 miles, the trail reaches the original junction of the day. A left turn here follows the stick of the lollipop back to the trailhead.

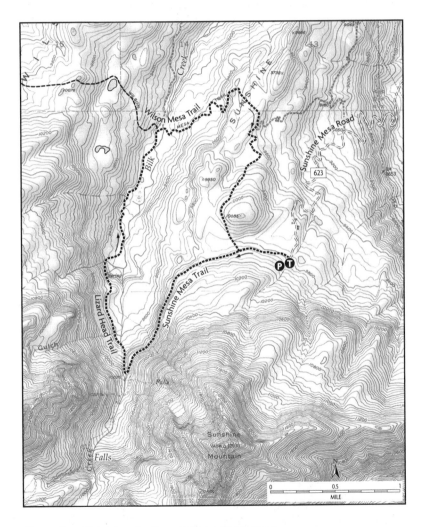

Opposite: Old mine shaft on Wilson Mesa Loop

43 | PORTLAND TRAIL

Round trip ■	**3.5 miles**
Loop direction ■	Counterclockwise
Hiking time ■	2.5 hours
Sweat factor ■	Low+
Starting elevation ■	8230 feet
High point ■	9210 feet
Low point ■	8230 feet
Elevation gain ■	1050 feet
Best hiking season ■	June through October
Maps ■	USGS Ouray
Contact ■	Uncompahgre National Forest

Driving directions: To get here, head south from Ouray on US 550 for 1.5 miles and turn east at the entrance to the Amphitheater Campground. Cruise up this paved road for 1.1 miles, past the campground, to the trailhead at the end of the road.

The quaint mountain town of Ouray boasts some of the most dramatic terrain in the state, and along with the lofty beauty is a rich history underground. The Portland Mine burrowed into the rock in the rugged mountains above Ouray, and today the well-maintained Portland Trail takes hikers on a mellow journey through rich and verdant forest and hugs the edge of a deep valley flanked by a grand amphitheater of beauteous alpine scenery. This epic mountain cirque rises nearly 4000 feet higher than the tiny town below! The trail follows mostly gentle grades, and braids of streams fall down the slopes of the massive bowl, their soothing songs echoing throughout this high-altitude arena.

This short loop starts by slanting steeply away from the parking lot, forging southwest through pine and short shrubbery as we head toward the Uncompahgre Gorge. At the trail's first curve, we are treated to glimpses of the impressive walls and cirques that enfold Ouray. If ever there was an archetypal mountain town, surely this is it. It's difficult not to just stop and stare—what a beautiful place. At 0.2 mile, we arrive at the first junction and hike straight and south toward the indicated Portland Trail. The soft dirt trail

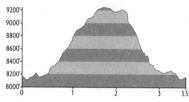

descends for another tenth of a mile before reaching intersection number two. Let's veer left, toward Portland Trail 238, and switchback down into and right out of a creekbed. Heading north now, we'll find our last junction of confusing consequence at 0.5

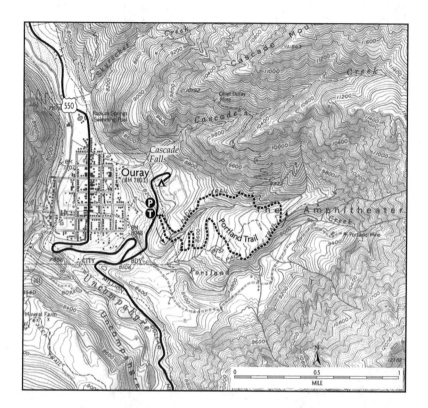

mile and turn left to the "official" start of the Portland Trail. Just navigating our way to this point may prove more difficult than the hike itself! But we're on our way now.

Heading east, we begin a long, steady ascent of enormous switchbacks. Each time we reach the southern tips of these large zigzags, more and more of the Amphitheater reveals itself to the east, and to the west rises the burly beginning of the Sneffels Range. Our path continues in and out of beautiful glades of pine and aspen until the switchbacks end and the trail follows a steadier course to the northeast.

At just over 1.5 miles, a rest stop is already a good idea. It is somewhat disconcerting, and impressive at the same time, that this hike is one of the mildest in the area. These mountains command respect, and show no quarter to the faint of heart. Let's take a breather on this bluff, with fantastic views of castle-like spires jutting high off the top of the Amphitheater, and echoes of distant waterfalls. Past the bluff, the trail winds through a dense pine forest and flirts with the edge of the mammoth canyon between here and the Amphitheater. At 2 miles, we have reached the high point in the hike; out to the east, the top of the ridge looks like thousands of enormous turrets. We'll take a left at the

Wind-blown Gambel oaks on the Portland Trail

next junction and begin the long descent toward the campground, winding deep into the pines across a creek to a west-facing slope with more spectacular views of the surrounding mountains. The junction with the Upper Cascade Falls Trail at 2.5 miles offers an extra challenge for those with the time and inclination. A right turn here leads up past Upper Cascade Falls to the old Chief Ouray Mine, a solid 1000 vertical feet above. While the rewards for that effort would be great, let's keep this hike a bit easier and continue straight through both this junction and the next, following the Upper Cascade Falls Trail down to the west.

Hiking southwest back toward the trailhead, we are enveloped by waves of wind-blown Gambel oak trees arcing majestically over the trail. We've made it to the end of the loop at 3.1 miles, and a right turn leads back to the parking area. Now it's time to head down for lunch and general lazing about in Ouray.

44 OAK FLAT LOOP

Round trip ■	**1.2 miles**
Loop direction ■	Counterclockwise
Hiking time ■	45 minutes
Sweat factor ■	Low
Starting elevation ■	8160 feet
High point ■	8160 feet
Low point ■	7760 feet
Elevation gain ■	400 feet
Best hiking season ■	May through October
Maps ■	USGS Grizzly Ridge; National Park Service, Black Canyon of the Gunnison
Contact ■	Black Canyon of the Gunnison National Park

Driving directions: Black Canyon of the Gunnison National Park is located 7 miles north of US 50 on Colorado 347. Plenty of signage on the roads makes it easy to find. Pay the entrance fee and follow the road to the visitor center. The trail begins right outside the door on the west side of the building. Let's go check it out!

"No other canyon in America combines the depth, narrowness, sheerness, and somber countenance of the Black Canyon of the Gunnison." A keen observation from geologist Wallace Hansen, and a thought shared by many who have peered into the depths of this amazing canyon. Designated national park status in 1993, 14 miles of the 48-mile-long canyon is now within the park. South Rim Drive provides numerous viewing points into different sections of this gorge, including the spectacular Painted Wall and Warner Point, the canyon's deepest location. There are a few short hiking trails along the south rim, one of them being this loop adjacent to the visitor center. It is a short trek just below the rim, with two overlooks and dazzling views.

A sign for the Oak Flat Trail leads

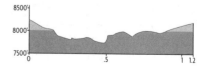

us on hard-packed tread into a stand of Gambel oak. There are great views of the North Rim way over there, and Painted Wall is visible upstream. Stroll down a gradual descent to a right turn at a sign for Oak Flat Trail and River Access. While this is a short and nontechnical trail, it drops 400 feet below the rim, then climbs right back up, so keep that in mind. This is a fun hike with the chance to get up close with the wilderness and leave the tourist crowds and walkways behind. We'll wander down through piñon pine, juniper, and even some aspen to the junction with the River Access Trail. With a permit, this path will allow access to the floor of the canyon, nearly 2000 feet below.

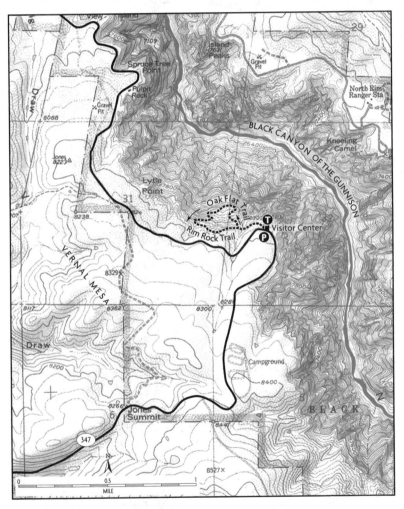

Opposite: Piñon pine at the Black Canyon

It is an excellent destination for backcountry camping. We will stay on the main trail, approaching a big rock outcrop with sweet views of the canyon walls in both directions. The gorge is dark and ominous, and is named for that reason. It is so deep, and so narrow at the bottom, that only faint sunlight can permeate the shade.

After the overlook, our trail climbs back into a forest of Douglas-fir, aspen, and Gambel oak. After a few switchbacks, we have regained some elevation and can see more of the canyon walls on the north side. We will pass through aspen and pine, and cross a few little wooden bridges to a final junction with the Rim Rock Trail. We keep on straight ahead, back through the scrub oak and a relaxing stroll to the trailhead.

Did you know:

- The Gunnison River loses more elevation on its journey through the Black Canyon's 48 miles than the Mississippi River does in 1500 miles?
- Prior to the construction of upstream dams, the river roared through the canyon at sustained flood stage—12,000 cubic feet per second and 2.75 million horsepower of force? That speed and violent energy scoured the gorge for two million years to create what we see today.
- At Warner Point, the canyon is a whopping 2772 feet deep?
- Although the canyon appears unforgiving and harsh, it supports vibrant plant and animal life, from the rims high above all the way to the bottom of the river? Look for great horned owls, Steller's jays, and mountain bluebirds near the rims. Peregrine falcons, swifts, and canyon wrens live and feed along the canyon walls. Water ouzels and weasels can be found near the river, and the river itself boasts a healthy fish population.

WESTERN SLOPE AND CANYONLANDS

45 DEVILS CANYON LOOP

Round trip ■	**6.5 miles**
Loop direction ■	Clockwise
Hiking time ■	3.5 hours
Sweat factor ■	Moderate
Starting elevation ■	4580 feet
High point ■	5198 feet
Low point ■	4403 feet
Elevation gain ■	670 feet
Best hiking season ■	Year-round
Maps ■	USGS Mack
Contact ■	Bureau of Land Management, Grand Junction Field Office

Driving directions: To reach the Devils Canyon trailhead, turn south off of Interstate 70 at the Fruita exit. Drive 1.5 miles on Colorado 340 and turn right (west) into the Kings View Estate subdivision. Proceed for 1.3 miles before turning left at a small sign indicating the Devils Canyon trailhead. Follow this road to the dead end (about 0.2 mile) to reach the trailhead.

On the extreme western side of Colorado, there is a primeval desert land of astounding beauty. With painted canyon walls, massive columns of rock, and open red valleys dotted green with sage, juniper, and piñon pine, these colorful canyonlands take hikers into a world of desert splendor. The Devils Canyon Loop follows a narrow river gorge full of terraced waterfalls, cupped sandstone cliffs, and slickrock ledges en route to a world of head-high junipers and rabbitbrush set against red and purple walls rising hundreds of feet above. Nourished by the nearby Colorado River, the bowels of the canyon are home to panthers, bighorn sheep, rabbits, and peregrine falcons. This area is also home to some of the harshest weather conditions in the state. During the summer, the temperature often climbs above 100 degrees. The Bureau of Land Management recom-
mends carrying a gallon of water per person per day. Conversely, during the winter, temperatures can dip

below freezing and snow is common. Enjoy this spectacular area, but be prepared for the elements.

Our trek on this lollipop loop begins by wandering southwest over a wide gravel and dirt path accessible to hikers and horses. Ubiquitous piñon pine and Utah junipers speckle the red landscape creating the beautiful mosaic characteristic of this desert country. As the trail turns south along a muddy tributary creek of the Colorado River, it passes small sandstone formations

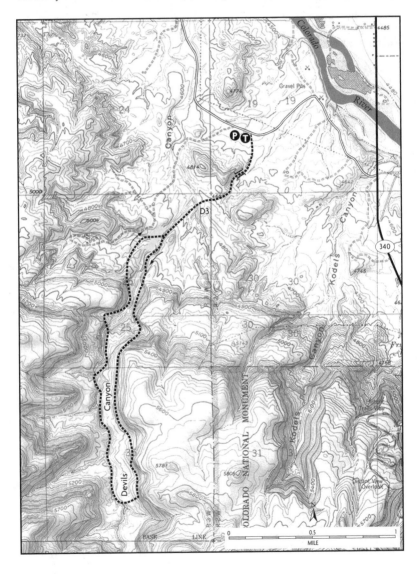

Shallow stream winding through Devils Canyon

foreshadowing the massive canyon ahead. A bridge crosses the creek to a junction at 0.25 mile. We'll continue south in the direction of Trail D1 as rolling buttes introduce the start of the high canyon walls.

We slowly lose some elevation as the trail wanders southeast, and at 0.4 mile stay left and walk toward D2, D3, and K1. Soon after, the sign indicating D3 appears and we'll veer right and enter a narrow gully following the creek all the way to the beginning of the canyon. The dirt trail gives way to rock hopping as we continually cross the creek in our southern pursuit. The meandering chocolate milk–colored water has created smooth alcoves and erratic bends in the red and yellow stone. The water glides soothingly over broad slabs of rock and is squeezed into myriad small waterfalls on its insistent voyage to the

Colorado River. Juniper, sage, and saltbush add their own color to the scene. As we approach 1 mile, the gully opens up and we continue heading south past the junction with D4 into the Black Ridge Canyons Wilderness.

After a few more crisscrosses with the creek, we officially begin the Devils Canyon Loop at 1.2 miles. Let's stay left to hike clockwise and begin climbing into the mouth of Devils Canyon. From the split, we begin a hearty climb up through the junipers and into the canyon, with humbling red walls rising like medieval castles on both the east and west sides. Be sure to look behind for great views to the north of the Book Cliffs. There are gravity-defying minarets of rock all over in this area, looking like they could tumble any minute now. The trail slowly rises, but consistently undulates through head-high piñon and juniper, all the while moving south in and out of secondary drainages feeding the creek. At close to 3 miles in, the trail makes a quick drop to the right as it reaches the far end of the loop, descending between layers of red and fuchsia rocks down to the muddy creek and just as quickly rising out on the western side of the canyon to begin the return trek. We'll pass by a small hut and turn north, wandering back toward the canyon mouth. There are more drainages on the west side of the canyon, and more breaks in pthe wall creating deeply cut cirques and smaller side canyons. At 5 miles, the creek pops back into view on our right as we begin a steep descent alongside a beautiful, striped wall. After the trail bottoms out at the base of this wall, we'll follow the creek to the sign indicating the beginning of our loop at 5.25 miles. Let's do a little more river running and rock hopping as we follow the stem of the loop back to the trailhead.

46 ┊ POLLOCK BENCH TRAIL

Round trip ■	5.5 miles
Loop direction ■	Counterclockwise
Hiking time ■	3 hours
Sweat factor ■	Moderate
Starting elevation ■	4496 feet
High point ■	5243 feet
Low point ■	4495 feet
Elevation gain ■	967 feet
Best hiking season ■	Year-round
Maps ■	USGS Mack
Contact ■	Bureau of Land Management, Grand Junction Field Office

Driving directions: To reach the Pollock Bench trailhead, follow Interstate 70 to the Fruita exit. Drive 1.5 miles on Colorado 340 and turn right (west) into the Kings View Estate subdivision. Continue for 3.5 miles to the trailhead on the left side of the road.

When people think of Colorado, the state's magnificent mountain ranges traditionally take all the credit. And deservedly so—Colorado owns the highest average elevation in the country, and its alpine acreage is nothing short of magical. Ah, but secret treasures in out-of-the-way locales are testament to just how diverse this beautiful state truly is. Far to the west are magnificent painted canyons, vast mesas, and deep winding gorges offering a playground to desert lovers. The Pollock Bench Loop in the Black Ridge Canyons Wilderness follows a long, curving cliff face, moves through dense junipers and piñon, and offers terrific views of the "forgotten" canyons in western Colorado.

This lollipop hike delivers the goods right from the start. A junction in the trail appears only a few dozen steps from the trailhead, and we turn right toward the sign indicating Trail P1—all of the trails in the area are labeled with this letter/number combination. P1 ascends a wide clay and dirt path with humbling views. To the south, the imposing walls of Devils Canyon rise out of the landscape like sphinxes. Behind us to the east, the massive wall of the Book Cliffs follows a ragged bearing toward Grand Junction and the Grand Mesa beyond. The trail leads to the top of a small knoll with views of the Colorado River lazily meandering westward. We'll pass through a small gate and at 0.4 mile arrive at the start of the loop. Turn right here, again toward P1, and follow the trail counterclockwise, climbing into the wilderness area. This new (in 2000) wilderness area straddles the Colorado-Utah border is a stunning 75,000-acre collection of red rock canyons, high cliffs, waterfalls, and mesas. Black Ridge is the highlight, as well as seven magical canyon systems chock full of tall spires, caves, and a gaggle of hidden spur canyons. Some of these ravines plunge to 1000 feet deep and roam hither and yon for 12 miles! If that's not enough, the wilderness also boasts the second largest collection of natural arches in the nation, second only to Utah's Arches National Park.

The trail travels across slate rock on its way to the crest of another small knoll, turning west on top of this bench cliff and following its contours. White and red stone dominate the area, pocked by green dots of piñon pine, Utah juniper, and sagebrush. The upland mesas are home to sage and grass meadows, as well, in stark contrast to the riparian foliage in the drainages below. Wildlife is also abundant throughout the area—look for mountain lions, desert bighorn sheep, bald eagles, deer, and a lot more.

Walking along the path through jumbles of broken rocks, look carefully at the walls that create the ledge. Wind is a tireless artist that creates portraits of smooth lines

and graceful curves on canvasses of rock, like these large escarpments blushed red and orange, tinged with strokes of faded white, and splashed with caramel. The colors seem to radiate from the stone and the place just feels good all over. Soon the trail curves southwest and begins another short ascent up more terraced sandstone formations to another canyon. From here, the path continues to rise over rockier tread to the top of this plateau and another junction at 1.5 miles. A right turn here provides access to Rattlesnake Canyon, a longer hike into the enchanting lands of the aforementioned arches country; let's keep moving straight ahead on a southwesterly course. Tall juniper and piñon briefly obscure the nice views, but before long we burst from the trees on the southern side of the plateau to greet more impressive vistas of sprawling canyons below. Another junction arrives at 2.6 miles, and we head east now onto Trail F2, descending along a few mild switchbacks toward the mouth of Flume Creek Canyon.

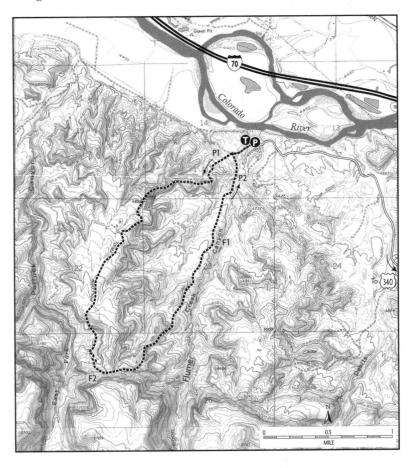

Rock shelf in desert country

A massive sandstone wall on our left flanks the trail as we head down through several minor drainages, eventually wandering onto a large slickrock marked with cairns. Up ahead, a monstrous cube of rock defying any sensible notion of balance is perched on top of a ledge of stone. It's one of those that looks like you could walk over and give it a little shove and send it tumblin' down the canyon.

The trail descends to the bottom of this ledge of rock to 3.1 miles and a left turn (northeast) toward Trail F1, meandering over cracked red clay through scattered juniper. Keep your eyes peeled for cairns and a well-trodden trail as washes tend to create a number of phantom routes. After paralleling a few more walls and outcroppings of rock, the original ledge we followed pops out to the left across this large, open mesa. The trail becomes something of a road with sweeping, 360-degree vistas of these huge canyons. At 4.7 miles, the trail leads out of the wilderness area, and only a short way farther is a left turn at a junction and a sign leading to Trail F1. Approaching 5 miles, we will pass through a fence and take a right at the next junction toward Trail P2 and an ascent to the end of the loop.

47 ¦ MARY MOORE LOOP

Round trip ■	9.5 miles
Loop direction ■	Counterclockwise
Hiking time ■	5 hours
Sweat factor ■	Moderate+
Starting elevation ■	4590 feet
High point ■	5329 feet
Low point ■	4584 feet
Elevation gain ■	1425 feet
Best hiking season ■	Year-round
Maps ■	USGS Mack; BLM area maps
Contact ■	Bureau of Land Management

Driving directions: To reach the beginning of the hike, drive west from Grand Junction on Interstate 70. Turn south at the Loma exit and take a right onto the frontage road and then a left toward the Kokopelli trailhead. Follow the road up and over a small hogback and down to a parking area just past the Moore Fun trailhead. On busy days, it may be necessary to park at the larger Kokopelli trailhead and walk to the beginning of the loop.

This trail is a combination of the Moore Fun Trail and Marys Loop in the Colorado Canyons National Conservation Area west of Grand Junction. This wonderful trail climbs to the top of a small mountain with panoramic views of much of the Colorado River basin in the western reaches of the state, with glimpses toward the Book Cliffs, the Grand Mesa, and the Black Ridge Canyons Wilderness. Part of the trail travels right next to the mighty Colorado River and follows a colorful sandstone cliff along a wide, open mesa. The trails are a part of the mountain bike–inspired Kokopellis Loop Trail Area. As this is a multiuse area, be sure to respect all the users of the trails and have fun out here.

This hike begins by heading west on the Moore Fun Trail into a rocky valley. On our left, a ridgeline covered with yucca, shrubs, and junipers obscures an open vista that we will revisit later on. The trail alternates between single- and double-track as it winds its way through this valley, up

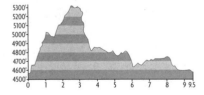

over small dirt mounds, and down into washes. Intermittent signs mark the path, and soon we ascend into the rocky bluffs, passing low-lying foliage and large chunks of rock poking out of the hillside every which way. We'll make one big switchback,

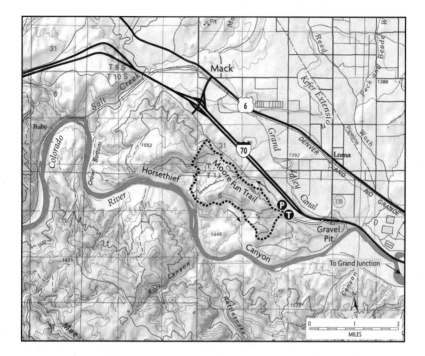

which allows views east toward Fruita, Grand Junction, and the Grand Mesa. The variegation of colors in the area is truly amazing, with large talus, stunted trees, an occasional creek, and sandstone everywhere. At 1.1 miles, the path climbs out of the rocky landscape onto a flat basin and turns north on a wide arc through the valley. Now on the northern side of the ridge, there are glimpses down toward Interstate 70 and the pastoral land leading all the way out to the high walls of the Book Cliffs. From here, we turn back left and start switchbacking up this hillside to the southwest. Then, almost unexpectedly, we top out on this mountain at 2.3 miles to splendiferous views! Enormous canyons run from east to west with curving mesas set in front of them. The Book Cliffs to the north look like an impenetrable fortress, and the land to the east slowly rises out to the plateau. The soft yellow dirt trail follows the ridgeline west, with a few small knolls covered with juniper and purple rocks. Soon the Colorado River comes into view, snaking just below a long, red cliff face. The rocky trail turns back to the right, descending along switchbacks through juniper and huge boulders. After the main section of switchbacks, the trail wraps northwest and comes down flush with a fence at 4.2 miles. We follow this fence for a bit before passing through a gate and continuing down to the end of the Moore Fun Trail.

At the next junction, let's go left onto the Marys Loop Trail by crossing over the cattle guard and descending into a huge valley. Following a double-track

Juniper on the Moore Fun Trail

road that splits, the trail chases signs for Marys Loop, descending deeper into the valley. In the heart of the valley, we wind by a pond and down into and out of drainages. Slowly, we rise out the valley to the grandeur of the Black Ridge Canyons Wilderness just to the south of the sweeping Colorado River. As the hike approaches 6 miles and the junction with the Steves Loop Trail, Marys Loop emerges right above the river. Before its departure from the state, the river softly flows beneath a long peach and red escarpment of sandstone, above which canyon walls tower majestically. We'll move southeast and parallel the river for a while on a single-track trail that leads up and down through a number of drainages and follows the contours of the hills on this rocky overlook. The path passes through a gate and tracks along the top of this long bench of solid rock, with a view of the high point in the hike to the left. At 7.9 miles, we pass the junction with the Horsethief Bench Loop, meander along toward the end of the rim, and descend rapidly en route to the beginning of the loop. At 9.3 miles, we meet back up with the road to the trailhead and it is just a short stretch to go to the conclusion of another fantastic hike.

NORTHERN MOUNTAINS

48 WALL LAKE LOOP

Round trip ▪	**14 miles**
Loop direction ▪	Counterclockwise
Hiking time ▪	10 hours
Sweat factor ▪	High+
Starting elevation ▪	9610 feet
High point ▪	11,290 feet
Low point ▪	9610 feet
Elevation gain ▪	2180 feet
Best hiking season ▪	June through September
Maps ▪	USGS Trappers Lake
Contact ▪	White River National Forest, Flat Tops Wilderness

Driving directions: To get here, take Interstate 70 to Rifle and head north on Colorado 13 for 40 miles to the town of Meeker. Continue for 1 mile past Meeker, then turn right and head east on Rio Blanco County Road 8 for 39 miles. Turn southeast onto Trappers Lake Road (Forest Road 205) for 11 miles. Finally, just before Trappers Lake Lodge, look for signs pointing to the right, across a creek to the campgrounds and trailheads. Follow the road past the campgrounds and look for the Wall Lake trailhead on the right.

This epic loop is nestled in the Flat Tops Wilderness Area, the second largest wilderness area in the state. Highlighting the unique Flat Tops landscape is an enormous plateau that was sculpted by a long-ago ice age. The hike begins at Trappers Lake, crosses through three massive valleys, descends through a long, cliff-enclosed valley, and climbs up onto one of the massive flattop mountains. How's that for a full day? There are two beautiful lakes that offer great camping and fishing, and the soft sounds of creeks making up the headwaters of the White River. If these laurels aren't enough, the hike also boasts some of the most brilliant and abundant wildflowers we have ever seen. Plan to visit in the spring when the flowers are dressed to the nines.

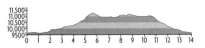

We will set out on Wall Lake Trail 1818 and move southwest though the widespread remnants of the Big Fish fire that swept the area in 2002. As a direct result of the fire, thousands of magenta fireweed and yellow butter-cups blanket the burn area. On a bright, sunny morning, with blue skies, blackened trees, and the vibrant colors of the flowers, this first stretch of the hike is classic Colorado. We'll wander over and between small, rolling hills and ramble past Anderson Lake through stop-in-your-tracks scenery; it is hard to imagine anything else on this trek can compare to the beauty

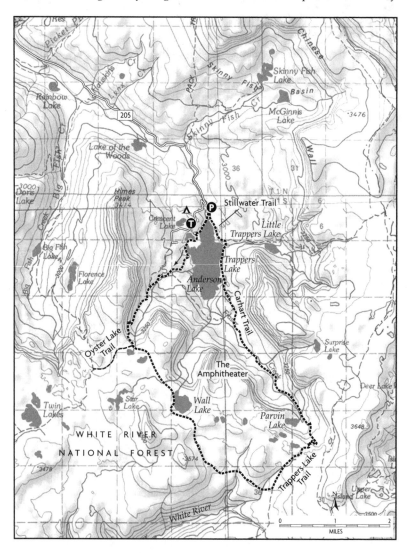

right in this spot. Believe it or not, there is much, much more!

Gradually gaining elevation, this single-track dirt trail wanders in and out of the burn and nice views of Trappers Lake appear to the northeast. As we amble south, massive walls and cirques crowd in, and we cross a few footbridges over snow-fed creeks trickling down from above. The path leads to the western side of this valley and climbs up the sunny, east-facing wall approaching the headwall of this flattop mountain. After moving a bit farther south, our first junction arrives with a complement of breathtaking views. At 2.75 miles, Oyster Lake Trail 1825 meanders off to the right. We'll stay left and continue on Trail 1818 to the southeast. Immediately in our path are four glorious pothole lakes glistening blue in the sun. These unnamed ponds rest in a vast valley of verdant tundra that leads south out to Trappers Peak. Continuing on toward Wall Lake, we are up on one of these flattop mountains now, trekking southeast on a level, treeless plateau. The dirt trail cruises past some low-lying shrubs and we are treated to uninhibited views of this high, pristine wilderness area. After crossing over a couple of creeks at the low points of this valley, we reach Wall Lake at 4 miles. A crumbling wall of rocks on the southern and eastern sides flanks this aptly named lake, while timbered areas of spruce and fir provide great hideaways for tents. Views from this beautiful lake look out north over an awesome valley called the Amphitheater, which stretches to the southern reaches of Trappers Lake.

The trail climbs up on top of the wall of crumbly rocks on the southern end of the lake, cruising along a smooth dirt path and squeezing over a low-lying pass at 4.8 miles. We soon greet a new and equally splendid valley extending eastward, speckled with dozens of pothole ponds on a landscape akin to a wild Alaskan basin. This place has the feel of bear country, and if you keep your eyes peeled, you just might spot one amidst the brush or along the shores of one of the lakes. The trail descends from the pass on the southwest side of this immense valley, revealing views to more dome-shaped mountains in the distance. We'll pass over a couple of drainages and begin to wind eastward, leaving this valley and entering yet another as we approach mile 6. The path loops and bends through another area chock-full of colorful wildflowers and spruce trees, and over several creeks that are the uppermost headwaters of the South Fork of the White River. After curving south of this 500-foot knoll, the Wall Lake Trail ends and we join the Trappers Lake Trail 1816 at 7.1 miles. Let's go left and begin the ascent leading toward the high point in the hike. Moving northeast now, the trail works its way into stunning high alpine landscapes of the headwaters creeks and more miniature ponds around each bend. As the trail flirts with tree line, we are rewarded with fantabulous views of the area, including gnarled krummholz trees, the durable, high-altitude trees that face a constant barrage of fierce winds and other unfriendly weather conditions. At 8.1 miles, continue straight to the northwest on Trappers Lake Trail 1816 (a right turn leads toward the West Mountain Trail). A large flattop adorned with an even higher dome of rock like a derby hat dominates the view to the east, and as

Gone fishin' in the Flat Tops

the route pushes north, it enters a massive, carved-out valley speckled with myriad rock-embraced ponds.

The trail switchbacks down into a heavily wooded area with beautiful views of Trappers Lake to the northwest. Parvin Lake sneaks into view between the trees along the descent through the middle of this massive valley. The landscape becomes laden with black ghosts of trees and beautiful flowers. At 9.2 miles, the trail wanders past the eastern side of Parvin Lake to a steady northwest descent following Fraser Creek. At 11 miles, the Trappers Lake Trail ends and the Carhart Trail 1815 leads off in two directions. Let's stay right and north along the eastern side of the lake, descending between a cluster of knolls. The trail works north following the shape of the shore to 13 miles, crossing the river rushing down from Little Trappers Lake—or rather, the river crosses the trail. There is more than adequate potential to get wet at this crossing. Shortly after, the trail meets up with Stillwater Trail 1814, where we'll turn left and continue north to the outlet of the lake. Follow the shore of the lake to the wooden bridge that crosses the outlet on the northern tip. The bridge offers wonderful views south toward the symmetrical, rising valley that makes up the Amphitheater. From here, the trail works southwest before a short climb back up to the trailhead. Walk out of the parking lot and 0.2 mile away on the left is where we began this unforgettable journey.

49 GILPIN LAKE LOOP

Round trip ■	10.5 miles
Loop direction ■	Clockwise
Hiking time ■	6 hours
Sweat factor ■	High
Starting elevation ■	8400 feet
High point ■	10,828 feet
Low point ■	8400 feet
Elevation gain ■	2417 feet
Best hiking season ■	Late May through October
Maps ■	USGS Mount Zirkel
Contact ■	Routt National Forest, Mount Zirkel Wilderness

Driving directions: To reach the trailhead, drive 2 miles west of Steamboat Springs on US 50 before turning right and driving north on County Road 129. After 18 miles, turn right onto Seedhouse Road (Forest Road 400 or County Road 64) and continue 11 miles to the Slavonia trailhead at the end of the road. Signs are posted for the trail.

The Mount Zirkel Wilderness Area extends long and narrow into the northern reaches of the state, and boasts rugged, rocky peaks of the Continental

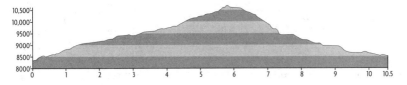

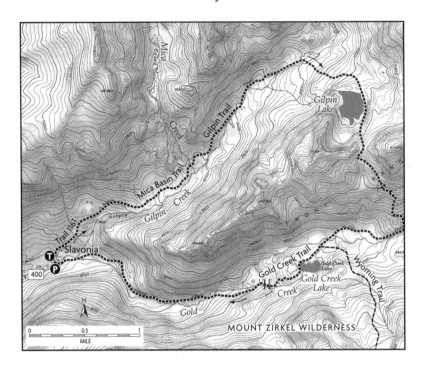

Divide and large forests of pine and aspen. This hike wanders about in these forests and visits a high, lonely lake along the way. The path affords terrific views of Mount Zirkel, the highest point in the area, and takes hikers over the top of a pass for a long and excellent day hike.

Our first steps on the trail take us northeast through an immense and dazzling stand of aspen. At 0.1 mile, there is a trail register; we'll sign in and turn left toward Trail 1161. A mellow climb brings us above one of a few beaver dams found along the hike. The dams create a number of drainages that trickle over the trail to feed Gilpin Creek below to our right. The trail becomes rockier at times as it climbs up this valley through aspen, Douglas-fir, and Engelmann spruce. There are glimpses south of the burned trees left by the Hinman fire of 2002. At 1.1 miles, the trail officially wanders into the Mount Zirkel Wilderness, one of the northernmost wilderness areas in the state and one of the original five to be designated as Colorado wilderness (1964).

The trail teases Gilpin Creek for a while, then bypasses the Mica Basin Trail and continues northeast 1.4 miles to where it breaches a small plateau with fine views east to the Continental Divide and Mount Zirkel. At 1.7 miles is the confluence of Gilpin and Mica Creeks; shortly after this meeting, we cross over Mica. Delving into mile 2, the rocky trail makes a noticeable shift to the south-facing side of this expansive valley and makes a couple switchbacks as it steadily gains altitude to the northeast. The landscape is freckled with widespread trees and a number of boulders allowing for wonderful views to the mountain range in the east. The trail crosses another creek and heads east, passing mile 3 and entering the last expanse of the valley before pushing up to the lake. The path revisits Gilpin Creek again where a small waterfall spills down through this rocky gorge. We'll move away from the creek once more, cut east across the valley, and climb toward Gilpin Lake. Mount Zirkel, rising to 12,180 feet, stands just to the northeast amongst fellow monsters in this section of the Continental Divide.

A number of small drainages trickle over this steepest part of the trail and at last, at 4.2 miles, we reach the lovely Gilpin Lake. One of the more popular destinations in the wilderness, Gilpin is a perfect place to take a high-altitude rest stop. That cove of rock at the south end of the lake is our destination, so rest up here. After a nice break, let's follow the trail around the east side of Gilpin Lake toward the pass. The trail finds the base of a 40-foot cliff that pushes in the direction of the saddle and once on the south side of the lake, we'll switchback our way right up the heart of the pass. The entire way up,

Late fall sun shimmers on Gilpin Lake.

and certainly at the top, the views of the lake, the Continental Divide, and Mount Zirkel itself are all seen together for your first plenary snapshot of the day.

From the pass, the trail becomes a deep scar in the landscape as it leads us steeply south down the backside. After crossing over a few drainages and negotiating down a number of switchbacks, we come to the end of the Gilpin Trail 1161 at 5.8 miles. Now that we're at the far end of the loop, let's turn right and follow the Gold Creek Trail 1150 back west toward the beginning. We'll continue descending south through fir and lodgepole forests as the trail flirts with the enormous valley that separates us from the Continental Divide. Once the trail reaches the floor, we'll be turned west as we follow Gold Creek down the valley. The trail begins a steady and mellow descent in and out of copses of pines, and at 7 miles we'll cross the creek just before meeting the Wyoming Trail 1101. Continue straight on 1150 on this south-westerly course.

Soon after, we'll tread past Gold Creek Lake across flat land on the north side of the lake, with spectacular views east toward the Sawtooth Range. At the western end of the lake, we get another nice glimpse of the creek-forged valley before beginning the first of a few long switchbacks down into the forest. Continual meetings of unnamed creeks with Gold Creek result in the fast growth of this main artery. You can actually see the increase in water flow and intensity with each confluence. At 10.2 miles, we'll cross over a wooden bridge shortly before reaching the register marking the end of this amazing hike.

ROCKY MOUNTAIN NATIONAL PARK

50 | Gem Lake Loop

Round trip ▪	**10.8 miles**
Loop direction ▪	Clockwise
Hiking time ▪	5.5 hours
Sweat factor ▪	Moderate+
Starting elevation ▪	7741 feet
High point ▪	9210 feet
Low point ▪	7745 feet
Elevation gain ▪	2730 feet
Best hiking season ▪	Early May through October
Maps ▪	USGS Estes Park; Trails Illustrated, Rocky Mountain National Park
Contact ▪	Rocky Mountain National Park

Driving directions: From west of the junction of US 36 and US 34, take the first right and follow Devils Gulch Road north for just shy of 2 miles past the Stanley Hotel. The trailhead is simply a large turnout on the west side of the road. A small Gem Lake sign may or may not be posted. The Twin Owls trailhead option is a half-mile west, at the entrance to MacGregor Ranch. Either choice works for this loop, and the MacGregor trailhead has ample parking and restrooms, but we chose this option so as not to miss some especially gorgeous scenery right at the start.

The Gem Lake Trail is a fun day hike that travels through an idyllic valley, along a gurgling creek, and up to a magical mountain setting you won't soon forget. There are two trailheads for this hike, both of which are located off Devils Gulch Road, just north of Estes Park. Before going anywhere, we must stop at Shakes Alive! in Lower Stanley Village on US 34. Mary Liz and Joe are two of the nicest people in town and their charming little café serves up delectable treats, perfect for fueling up for a big day on the trail.

Rocky Mountain National Park

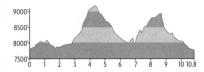

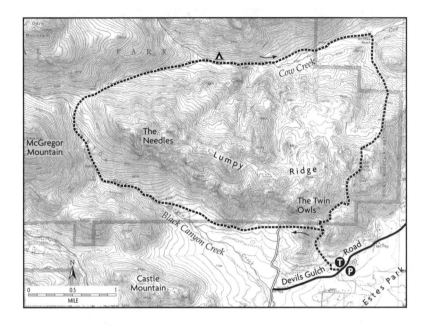

has been a jewel in the nation's park system since its induction in 1915. Joel Estes settled in the area in the mid-1800s, in the picturesque valley that embraces his namesake town of Estes Park. Notable visitors in later years, such as Isabella Bird and F. O. Stanley, had great influence on the area's future. And thanks to the tireless efforts of Enos Mills and others of like mind, the stunning grandeur of the surrounding mountains was preserved as the country's tenth national park. And what a park it is, with 360 miles of trail close at hand (or close at foot) to explore meadows and streams, valleys and forests, and magnificent high alpine tundra. Trail Ridge Road, the highest continuous paved road in the country, winds right up and over the Continental Divide, and at the top are decadent high-country scenes that leave visitors as breathless as the thin mountain air.

Gem Lake is a lollipop loop with a tiny handle and a huge hunk of candy. The first part of the handle is flat, and we'll follow it past a cluster of residential properties into a grove of petite aspen with a few pines scattered about. A slender creek trickles through here as well—we've barely started and already we're walking through a postcard. A turn or two in the path and a steady but gradual rise in elevation brings us to a sign announcing the official boundary of Rocky Mountain National Park. It somehow feels different stepping across the line into a park or wilderness area, as if simply taking that next step leads into some magical place. And this place feels enchanting indeed, with giant rocks morphed into all sorts of fantastical creations and fairy-tale trees growing from just a crack in the solid stone. At about 1 mile, we reach a junction and a sign pointing to the Twin Owls trailhead. We'll go left here to start the loop, with nice views of Estes Park and the mountains to the south. Around a curve and descending gently, a stop-in-your-tracks view opens to the west of the big mountains of the Continental Divide, and the bucolic landscape of MacGregor Ranch below. A gigantic rock needle towers just ahead as the path heads downhill past a spur trail leading to a climbing route on the neighboring rock.

We roll up to the Twin Owls trailhead at 1.5 miles. The trail continues on the other side of the parking lot, past the sign for Lawn Lake. Interpretive signboards stand along the trail here, loaded with fascinating details on the raptor species that call this place home. Break out your binoculars and ogle these majestic birds waltzing with the winds. We wander alongside a rustic split-rail fence toward Black Canyon Creek, then turn right through an opening in the fence, walking for a while on a strip of MacGregor Ranch. Elk are everywhere in the park—so common, in fact, that it would

Ancient natural amphitheater at Gem Lake

be a surprise *not* to see at least a few of them on this hike, especially in this pastoral meadow. To our right is Lumpy Ridge, a 1.8-billion-year-old spine of squishy-looking rock with individual, upright rocks called *tors*. The trail arrives at a gate (be sure to close it after passing through) that takes us back across the park boundary. We are roughly 3 miles into the hike and here the ground begins to tilt up as the ponderosa forest slowly gives way to lodgepole and fir. Get used to the steady grade—we get to enjoy it for over a mile, slogging upward between MacGregor Mountain to the west and The Needles to the east. The Needles are a jumble of primordial rock formations that aren't very needlelike at all—more like gigantic sausages sticking out of the ground.

At the 4-mile mark, there is a junction and the end of the first uphill grind. A left turn here heads 5 miles northwest to Lawn Lake, the culprit of a devastating flood that poured through Estes Park in 1982. We'll go right, up over one more ridge, and then finally head downhill, curving around a few switchbacks toward Cow Creek. Close to the bottom, the trail wanders through a vein of shimmering aspen and Cow Creek appears on the left. Continuing on, we stroll past an open, south-facing hillside with fine views of the not-so-lumpy side of Lumpy Ridge. The trail crosses Cow Creek as mile 6 comes along, and reaches another junction. A left leads to the beauteous Bridal Veil Falls, an excellent out-and-back day hike from the Cow Creek trailhead. At a little over 6 miles, just past the Rabbit Ears backcountry campsite, is another junction. This is a right turn for us, following the sign's lead to Balanced Rock, Gem Lake, and Twin Owls parking. Hiking out of the valley now, we cross over the creek again and begin an ascent up the north-facing side of Lumpy Ridge. The trail generally keeps to the contours of the mountain, but soon becomes steeper and demands more attention from already tired legs. Climbing higher, take a look behind for views of the southern edge of the Mummy Range. A short-lived plateau takes us past the trail to Balanced Rock, a fun side trip if you don't mind an extra couple of miles. One more stretch of uphill completes the eighth mile and brings us to aptly named Gem Lake. This is truly an amazing place—a tranquil lake cradled in a towering, two-billion-year-old amphitheater of rocks, with an attentive audience of ponderosa pine on the flanking slopes. It is simply impossible to just walk right through this scene, so allow extra time to soak it all in. But wait, there's a grand finale to this loop you're sure to love. Take a few more steps to the south end of the lake, to where a shallow stream of water falls lazily over the edge, and—behold!—a jaw-agape view of Longs Peak and various summits of the Continental Divide, plus the Estes Valley sweeping out below. What a spectacular end to this great hike.

A steep descent brings us back into the woods, with a couple of clearings that afford views of Lake Estes and the Stanley Hotel way down there, and the initial trail junction arrives at about 10 miles. Head left for the last mile back to the trailhead to finish the day.

51 | TRIPLE THREAT

Round trip	■	8 miles
Loop direction	■	Counterclockwise
Hiking time	■	7 hours
Sweat factor	■	High+
Starting elevation	■	11,164 feet
High point	■	13,514 feet
Low point	■	10,530 feet
Elevation gain	■	4185 feet
Best hiking season	■	June through October
Maps	■	USGS Trail Ridge; Trails Illustrated, Rocky Mountain National Park
Contact	■	Rocky Mountain National Park

Driving directions: Just getting to the trailhead is half the fun. From the Fall River Entrance Station to Rocky Mountain National Park, follow the road along Horseshoe Park to a right turn onto Old Fall River Road. Just past the Endovalley picnic area, the road turns to gravel and one-way. This is a truly memorable drive along the original route over the Continental Divide, with bird's-eye views of Trail Ridge and hold-your-breath looks over precipitous drops into Fall River's deep valley. Keep your eyes on the road for about 7 miles to the Chapin Pass trailhead and park in one of the turnouts. The trail starts on the north side of the road.

How about three summits on one great hike? This classic trek offers a full day of breathtaking high-altitude views along a mostly unmarked, above-timberline route. Beginning at the historic Old Fall River Road, the path climbs nearly without interruption to the rounded peaks of three very old mountains: Chapin, Chiquita, and Ypsilon. Unforgettable sights of distant high mountains, alpine ridges, and richly forested valleys lie in every direction, and the descent through primeval woods to Chapin Creek is a perfect finale to the trip. It is an arduous hike indeed, however, and just when you think it's over, the last stretch of trail climbs 520 feet in a half-mile. It is a chore just to lift your boots off the ground by this point, but it's worth every weary step.

The hike begins at Chapin Pass (11,164 feet) and immediately goes straight up a steep hill laced with gnarly roots and over rocks and logs and water bars. A lush stand of subalpine fir and Engelmann spruce shades the path. Already with these first few steps, a look behind reveals a fine view of the imposing Trail

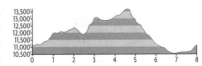

Ridge. At the top of this short climb, there is a sign announcing "Chapin, Chiquita, and Ypsilon Summits." We'll go thataway on the Chapin Pass Trail, heading on an easterly slant to higher ground. Just a couple of dozen steps take us through a narrow, open drainage with clear views of the three peaks awaiting our arrival. At about a quarter-mile into the hike, we ascend a rugged rock stairway through more spruce and fir. Great views open up of Chapin Creek Valley, below, and the Alpine Visitor Center atop the Continental Divide. The path breaks free of the trees and the three summits are dead ahead while the daunting Desolation Peaks loom from the north.

At just over a half-mile, we leave the last of the trees behind, following a moderate grade on the lower flanks of Mount Chapin, which is almost

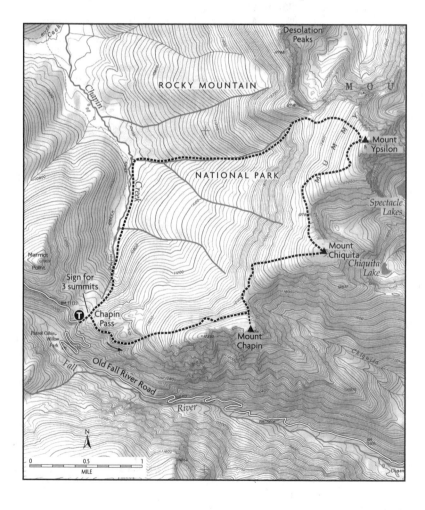

entirely covered with medium-size, flat-sided boulders. In the folds of the hill are numerous "rivers" of these angular rocks, rugged streambeds flowing only with the passage of time's inexorable hand. At a little over 1 mile we pass through a large talus field, and the trail becomes faint in a few places, but not enough to stray off course. Look for pikas darting among the rocks, chirping at our intrusion. We reach the saddle between Chapin and Chiquita and turn uphill toward the summit of Chapin and follow a well-marked cairn trail up a steeper grade. Take care with the fragile tundra foliage, stepping on the rocks when you can. The top of Mount Chapin (12,454 feet) is a big, rounded hump of rocks and alpine grasses and other flora. A rock shelter sits atop the crest, offering some relief from the fierce winds up here. The views are nothing short of stunning—Longs Peak rises high in the south, Estes Park is visible in the valley east, along with the plains farther out, the Never Summer mountains loom to the west, and our next two peaks are to the north.

We'll head back down from Chapin to the huge saddle leading up to Mount Chiquita. There is a cliff along the rim of the saddle that drops nearly straight down in a big hurry. It's a humbling sight to look over the edge, but do so carefully, a big gust of wind might nudge you just a little too close. The initial ascent of Chiquita is plenty steep, so be prepared to huff and puff. The trail is faint and at times disappears altogether, but our course generally follows the curve of the hill right to the top. An occasional cairn reminds us we're on track. The landscape is rockier closer to the top, but the grade levels a bit and we can recover some lost breath. Mount Chiquita's summit brings us to 13,069 feet, and the views just keep getting better. Right below the summit is a colossal crater cradling Lake Chiquita, and the sheer south face of Fairchild Mountain glares over Mount Ypsilon's shoulder. After a break in one of the three rock wind shelters, let's start the descent from Chiquita to another big saddle en route to our final summit. Rocks are everywhere on the "path" down, at times that's all there is to walk on, but pick a good line and be cautious of loose rocks; this is no place to twist an ankle. In no time we're at the edge of the saddle. Take a peek over the edge for an unforgettable, almost scary, view of the vertical drop below your boots. Ahead is the humbling sight of Mount Ypsilon and the long climb ahead.

The climb up Ypsilon is a steep trek along skinny paths on an immense field of rocks. There is a faint trail most of the way, and a few cairn markers offer reassurance. Farther up the hill, look for an extraordinary cliff face scrunched with squiggly striations of brown and beige and white. It looks like chocolate that's been melted with marshmallow. Excuse me a minute while I dig in my pack for some graham crackers. After just a few hundred more steps, we're at the summit of Mount Ypsilon at darn near 14,000 feet. Wow. There are dazzling, humbling, views of Spectacle Lakes below. Way, way down below. The Desolation Peaks stand tall to the northwest, and once again all other directions provide beautiful high-country vistas.

Heading for higher ground; Mounts Chiquita and Ypsilon to left

When it's time to descend, we'll do so through one of the drainages leading back to Chapin Creek. The one in the direction of Desolation Peaks is a good choice, so let's head that way, watching our step on the loose rocks on the way. It's rough going for a while here, with this side of the hill covered almost completely with angular boulders. But soon we are clear and back to tree line, entering a sublime world of gorgeous scenery with dense woods and a quiet stream drifting past moss-covered hillocks and dwarf foliage. A canopy of high branches of giant spruce and fir covers a tidy understory flushed with assorted shades of green, with white, blue, and pink wildflower accents. This is a great place to sit down and just listen, maybe even doze for a bit before the last miles of the hike.

We'll continue to follow the stream downhill to its confluence with Chapin Creek. Here at the edge of the woods is a wide band of soggy ground with the creek's main channel out there in the middle someplace. Our route turns south, climbing gradually uphill, and we will hike close to the trees on more solid turf to avoid damaging the fragile riparian landscape. At the head of the drainage is our final ascent. Back in the big trees, the trail tilts up posthaste, and it's not easy going after such a long day. Again, the scenery is simply gorgeous, if you can enjoy it through a fatigue-induced haze. Finally, the ground levels and we pass the summits sign and stumble down the last hill to the trailhead. Chalk up seven hours, 8 miles, and three peaks. What a great day.

52 | LITTLE MATTERHORN

Round trip ■	**16 miles**
Loop direction ■	Clockwise
Hiking time ■	1 to 2 days
Sweat factor ■	Moderate+
Starting elevation ■	8080 feet
High point ■	10,680 feet
Low point ■	8080 feet
Elevation gain ■	3226 feet
Best hiking season ■	Late June through October
Maps ■	USGS Estes Park; Trails Illustrated, Rocky Mountain National Park
Contact ■	Rocky Mountain National Park

Driving directions: We'll start from the Cub Lake trailhead, not far from the Beaver Meadows Entrance Station. To get there from the junction of US 34 and US 36 in Estes Park, follow US 36 south and west from town past the visitor center to the entrance station. Daily fees (in 2004) are $20 per vehicle and $10 for bicycles; and maps and more info are available here, too. Just past the entrance, turn left onto Bear Lake Road, which makes a couple of sweeping bends to the turnoff to Moraine Park. Turn right and follow this road to the Cub Lake and Fern Lake trailheads.

Here is a chance to enjoy a fabulous overnight trip in the center of Rocky Mountain National Park. Starting in the lush meadows of Moraine Park and skirting some impressive peaks at the base of the Continental Divide, this hike offers secluded lakes, numerous streams and rivers, waterfalls, and a big helping of some of the prettiest mountains in the park. Before we even take a single step, there are fine views of the high peaks of the Continental Divide to the west, a mighty backdrop to this peaceful valley. The Cub Lake Trail meanders over Big Thompson River and through an expansive riparian zone toward Steep Mountain. Look out into this

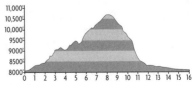

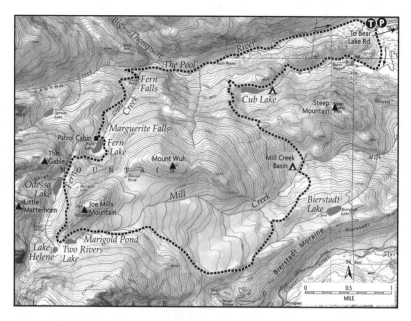

wetland meadow for signs of elk. This is a favorite hangout of theirs, so there is a good chance to spot a few.

After a short walk, the trail turns west and follows Cub Creek through stands of ponderosa and groves of willow. This is a nice path over gently rolling terrain as we leave these open areas and head into the trees. The grade steepens without hesitation into gorgeous deep woods, with small rivulets spilling over the trail. It's a pretty good climb on the way, passing the Cub Lake campsites, then Cub Lake itself appears over the next rise. The trail hugs the shoreline of this beautiful lake surrounded by woods with a high ridge at the west end and the big mountains of the Continental Divide beyond. We'll climb that ridge west of the lake, and from there we'll have a great view of Cub and its trademark necklace of lime-green lily pads.

At the top of the ridge, there is the junction with the trail leading to Fern Lake. We will be down that way tomorrow, so for now let's turn left and start climbing. This is a tough hill with about a mile of steep and rocky tread through lodgepole forest. When we finally reach the top there is a long descent on the other side on loose gravel into Mill Creek Basin, a beautiful narrow valley with stands of aspen and open meadows. Mill Creek tumbles rapidly through this valley. It's a lively stream with waterfalls and twists and turns on its way to meeting the Big Thompson River, and there happen to be a couple of fine backcountry campsites here, as well. Let's throw up a tent and soak in the beauty of this place for the night.

Opposite: Mill Creek Trail

Soft pink and purple light in the dawn sky offers a velvety promise of another perfect day, so with a spring in our step, we'll continue across the creek to a sign for Bear Lake, Bierstadt Lake, and Hallowell Park. This is a beauteous woods with big, gray boulders scattered about beneath fragrant pines. The trail turns away from the creek and climbs to the junction, at about 4.8 miles, with another path heading to Bear Lake. Our route goes this way, with even more long, steady climbing. Whew. There are good views of Mount Wuh to the north and glimpses of the stunning peaks around Bear Lake to the west and south. The trail crests a ridge and descends briefly on the other side to a fork at the Flattop Mountain Trail. Lean to the right here and begin a gradual climb toward tree line. After passing the split to Flattop Mountain, we wander into a gardenlike, alpine setting of lush grasses and the headwaters of Mill Creek. With an amazing view of Notchtop Mountain above it all, this is a perfect place to linger a while and rejuvenate.

After a break, our trail sneaks through another stretch of luxurious alpine scenery to a huge boulder field. Directly ahead is a jaw-agape view of the imposing Little Matterhorn. What a sight. The path heads right at it, and around a final turn the mountain looms tall, gray, and brawny. Waterfall tendrils veil vertical faces of the mountain, and smudges of green foliage add colors of life to the stern landscape. We turn north here, hugging close to the west flank of Joe Mills Mountain. Beware of the steep slope dead ahead. Two big snowfields we are about to cross cling to a steep, rocky slope, and a lot of melting and cooling changes the snow to hard-packed, slippery ice. Watch your step or it'll be time to go sledding.

Past the snow, the trail brings us closer to Odessa Lake, nestled in a narrow valley way down there. The view of the lake and the valley are quite nice from here, and the trail takes us closer, descending through a pretty landscape of dense pine and small streams reminiscent of the Oregon woods. We pass the junction with the trail to Odessa Lake at 9 miles. Fern Creek roars in the gorge to the left. Farther down, the trail curves past a giant boulder field and along the eastern shore of Fern Lake. Our path crosses the lake at a dam and Marguerite Falls, then travels past a park patrol cabin and back into the woods. From here, we enjoy a scenic walk downhill to Fern Falls thundering off a high, wooded cliff in a two-tiered cascade. A couple of switchbacks deliver us across a hummock with Fern Creek on one side and the Big Thompson River on the other, then around a corner to The Pool, a swirling cauldron of the Big T where it squirts between some huge boulders and a rock wall. A wooden bridge crosses this frothy maelstrom and directly on the other side is the junction with the Cub Lake Trail, leading back up to the lake and our early steps on this hike from yesterday. We'll veer left here and continue on the Fern Lake Trail, wandering through pretty stands of aspen and pine and past whimsical rock formations. The path is flat now and it is easy cruising to the parking area at the Fern Lake trailhead; from here, we simply follow the gravel road 0.8 mile to the Cub Lake trailhead to conclude this great hike.

53 | BIERSTADT LAKE LOOP

Round trip ■	**3.5 miles**
Loop direction ■	Counterclockwise
Hiking time ■	2+ hours
Sweat factor ■	Low+
Starting elevation ■	8855 feet
High point ■	9446 feet
Low point ■	8691 feet
Elevation gain ■	756 feet
Best hiking season ■	Late June through October
Maps ■	USGS Estes Park; Trails Illustrated, Rocky Mountain National Park
Contact ■	Rocky Mountain National Park

Driving directions: To get here, follow the same directions from the previous hike (Hike 52) to get to Bear Lake Road. Follow the road past the Moraine Park entrance to the Bear Lake shuttle parking area near Glacier Basin. Hop the shuttle and ride down to the Bierstadt Lake trailhead.

Bear Lake is one of the most popular destinations in Rocky Mountain National Park, and big crowds pour into the area by the busload. We typically avoid this type of scene at all costs, but the scenery here is so spectacular, we can't pass it up. Huge mountains flank a deep green valley, and cold, clear streams mosey through the woods. Bierstadt is a nice little trail conveniently located nearby where we can leave the tourists behind and explore a small part of Glacier Basin, and there is direct access to the Little Matterhorn hike, too.

At the trailhead, the sign for Glacier Basin Campground leads the way. The trail, on wide and smooth tread to start, heads northeast, paralleling the road, through stands of pine and aspen. After a short while the trail fades into a skinny, unimproved path, with little evidence of regular passage. It feels remote and primitive, even so close to the circus just down the road at Bear Lake. Strolling through this meadow of tall grasses, wildflowers, and slender aspen trees is a real treat, especially after a short, refreshing afternoon rain shower. At the first junction on the trail, there is a sign announcing Bierstadt Lake and Bear Lake; we'll hang a left here and begin a long steady climb. Finally reaching the top, the path levels and is almost flat to the next split with the trail that heads around Bierstadt Lake. This is the only chance to

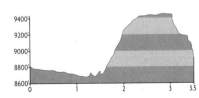

actually see the lake, as the main route skirts around it. Let's skip the lake and go right, on an easy stretch of trail to the junction with the Mill Creek Basin Trail. This is the way to go for access to Mill Creek and the Little Matterhorn hike (Hike 52), but we will go left to the Bierstadt Lake trailhead. Along the way is yet another split, this one being the western trail leading to Bierstadt Lake. Keep on truckin', through a beautiful setting of dense forest and lush understory. We have been walking atop the Bierstadt Moraine, a long glacial ridge with a steeply sloped southern wall. Arriving at the edge of this slope, we are rewarded with fantastic views of Hallet and Otis Peaks, and some of the other impressive mountains in this chunk of the Continental Divide. The trail begins a long chain of switchbacks, dropping into a shimmering stand of aspen with great views of the valley below and Sprague Lake over there to the east. Clearing the aspens, the path continues to descend through a section of open sage, then back into lodgepole forest

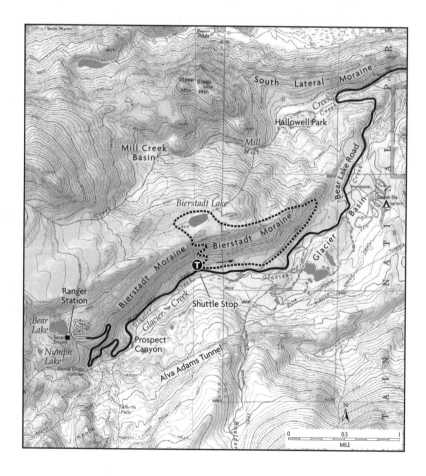

Elk at Mill Creek Basin

to the trailhead. The shuttle comes by here for a quick ride back, or retrace your steps to the Glacier Basin trailhead.

54 ONAHU CREEK TRAIL

Round trip ■	7 miles
Loop direction ■	Counterclockwise
Hiking time ■	4.5 hours
Sweat factor ■	Moderate+
Starting elevation ■	8826 feet
High point ■	10,230 feet
Low point ■	8823 feet
Elevation gain ■	1817 feet
Best hiking season ■	May through October, but snowshoe-accessible in the winter
Maps ■	USGS Estes Park
Contact ■	Rocky Mountain National Park

Driving directions: We'll start at the Green Mountain trailhead, located on US 34 approximately 3 miles past the Grand Lake Entrance Station on the western side of Rocky Mountain National Park.

This hike takes us over to the verdant west side of Rocky Mountain National Park. The trail begins in the massive Kawuneeche Valley, separating the high peaks of the Continental Divide and the Never Summer Wilderness. The trail leads through thick pine forests flecked with wildflowers and boulders. A northern stretch along the Long Meadows area affords dazzling views of the Divide, and there is a long descent through handsome forests guided by the enchanting music of a primitive creek.

We begin our hike on the Green Mountain Trail winding through a lovely mixed forest of pine, aspen, and spruce, heading east away from the trailhead. A small, gurgling creek following the trail plays softly to the ear, skipping lightly over petite waterfalls and through low shrubs and willow tufts. As the grade increases, so does the size of the stately lodgepole pines towering above our heads, and small basins open up to reveal neighboring mountains, like Green Mountain over there to the right. At 0.7 mile, the path crosses a collection of wooden bridges over a number of small drainages. Approaching 2 miles, the trail passes a small pond and veers north toward a large river valley flanked by 11,424-foot Mount Patterson. A junction appears, and we will take a left onto the Tonahutu Creek Trail in the direction of some backcountry campsites. At this point, we are situated on the edge of this high mountain meadow and its lush, riparian habitat; just beyond are the gnarled peaks of the Continental Divide nearly 3000 feet above our heads! The Little Matterhorn hike (Hike 52) and other loops we've done in eastern Colorado are just right over those big mountains; not that far as the white-tailed ptarmigan flies, but a full day of travel in a pair of boots.

We will continue north now along the left side of the massive basin of Tonahutu Creek. The trail moseys just inside the bordering wall of dense trees, offering broken views of the mountains out east. We'll pass a couple of ancient and dilapidated cabins situated right on the meadow's edge before the trail roller-coasters up and above the basin and right back down to it. So capturing and distracting are the views to the east, we hardly notice that once the undulating stops, the grade becomes rather arduous. At the junction at 2.7 miles, turn left toward the Onahu Creek trailhead and keep on climbing the steep grade north through this thick forest. After a lot of huffin' and puffin' by us, the trail tops out and snakes around a small knoll, then wanders over to a west-facing slope and cuts across a steep hillside pocked with rocky slopes and wildflowers. Check out the views to the west. Those huge mountains are part of the Never Summer Wilderness, and also contribute to the curving line of the Continental Divide. The mountains have lofty names like Mount Cumulus, Nimbus, and Cirrus and make up an ample portion of the park's far western border.

At 4 miles, we arrive at another junction. The Long Meadows Trail branches off to the right, but our path turns left here on the Onahu Creek Trail, shuffling across a small bridge over Onahu Creek and then

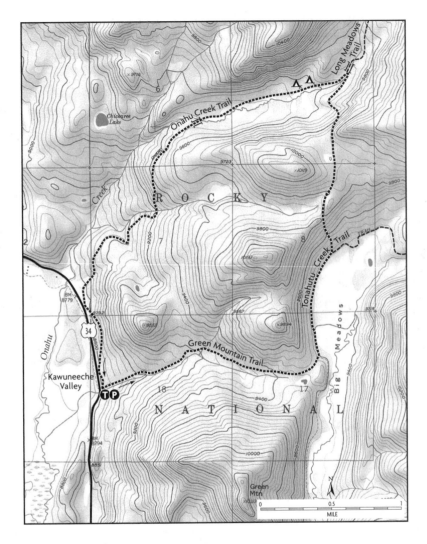

banking hard left in a westerly direction. The trail passes by two campsites, then parallels the creek, descending west here past mammoth boulders and into a wide, flat valley. Cheery wildflowers complement the scene as we amble along this easy grade with the sounds of the creek guiding our path. Keep your eyes peeled for a herd of elk or even a moose in here. The trail gets steeper as it turns southwest and soon we cross one of Onahu's main tributaries on a small bridge. From here, the path rises high above the echoing creek and meanders through more stands of giant lodgepole. There are some nice, last-minute views of the Never Summer Range, then the harsh

Never Summer mountains

presence of the highway comes into sight. We'll parallel the road down to the Onahu Creek trailhead, marking just a half-mile left in the hike. Turn left at the trailhead, back into the trees. For tired legs, the end to the hike may be something of a shock as the trail climbs up and down a series of hillocks before reaching the Green Mountain parking area and the conclusion of another fine hike in Rocky Mountain Park.

SNOWSHOE HIKES

55 POWDERHOUND TRAIL

Round trip	■ **2.75 miles**
Loop direction	■ Clockwise
Hiking time	■ 2.5 hours
Sweat factor	■ Low+
Starting elevation	■ 10,528 feet
High point	■ 10,672 feet
Low point	■ 10,411 feet
Elevation gain	■ 529 feet
Best hiking season	■ December through March
Maps	■ USGS Leadville North
Contact	■ San Isabel National Forest

Driving directions: To get to the trail, travel 9.75 miles northwest of Leadville on US 24 to Tennessee Pass. At the top of the pass are the Tenth Mountain Division Memorial and the entrance to Ski Cooper. The trailhead is directly across the highway from the entrance to the ski area.

How about a fun diversion from the traditional hike in the woods? Head for the mountains in winter, strap on a pair of snowshoes, and experience the high country's quiet, white solitude. In the high reaches of the San Isabel National Forest, a playful web of trails drapes right atop the Continental Divide. This short snowshoe hike makes use of both the Tree Line and Powderhound Trails to make one terrific loop that accommodates all abilities of snowshoers. The path wanders along two celebrated long-distance trails, the Continental Divide Trail and the Colorado Trail, as it climbs right over the Divide and makes a quick and fun descent through trees and valleys. It's a short, but rewarding trip, and is a perfect opportunity to get out there, especially when the snow is piling up.

Stop at the trailhead kiosk and grab a map before striking out west into this beautiful area. If you are first on the trail after a big snow and get to make first tracks, there are blue diamond markers along the way to keep you on course. The path gently rises through this thick stand of lodgepole pine, which instantly mutes traffic noise from the highway and it already feels like we are way out in the middle of isolated nowhere. There

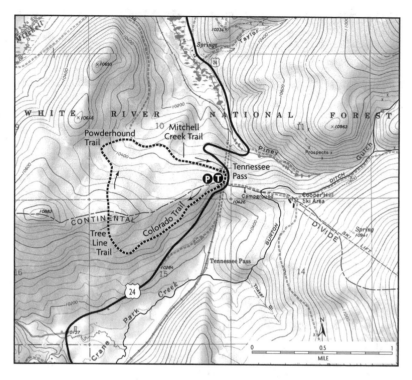

are two familiar trail symbols on the route, that of the Continental Divide Trail—extending for 3100 miles from the heights of Montana all the way to New Mexico—and the Colorado Trail, traveling more than 400 miles from Denver to Durango. This is distinguished terrain, indeed.

For wildlife activity, snowshoeing is a great opportunity to see hundreds of busy footprints skittering across the snow. Plan a trip after a fresh dump of snow, bring a guide to wildlife tracks, and enjoy some relaxing time identifying and following the myriad trails found in these woods—little ones weaving about with no particular place to go, bigger prints on an arrow-straight sprint for the cover of the boughs of a nearby pine. The trail undulates slightly down into drainages and back up hillsides as we move out onto a south-facing slope. Occasional breaks in the trees uncover nice outlooks south to the valley below and back east to Ski Cooper and its neighboring peaks. Up and down we go as the trail changes direction and turns south. Then at 0.7 mile, we'll say goodbye to the Colorado Trail and turn right toward the Tree Line Trail, which climbs up to the northeast.

Take a breather here before the most substantial climb of the day. The switchbacks up through the trees can be somewhat daunting in deep snow, so take it slow and enjoy the peace and quiet. A few steps past 1 mile take us to the junction with the Powderhound Trail. For a shorter loop, there is a bailout option on the trail that branches off to the right, but today let's continue straight to the north and begin the Powderhound. The trail ambles up over a knoll and crosses the Continental Divide. The trees around here are well spaced and healthy, and frame more magnificent views of the giant mountains that surround this pristine area. From the apex of the trail on the Divide, we descend through a variety of small open dells and secluded glades.

At 1.6 miles, the trail turns right and hooks back east. Keep out a sharp eye for the blue diamonds, as other hikers don't always heed the correct direction.

All alone on Tennessee Pass

One man's adventuresome footprints might be another's unexpected night in a snow cave. We'll move through some more seemingly impenetrable stands of lodgepole and out into another expansive valley with big views. Here, the trail intersects with the Mitchell Creek Trail. Let's turn right and follow this wider path back in the direction of the trailhead, gradually ascending again and passing into an open valley. From here, the views of Ski Cooper open up and behind us is a long-distance look at some big peaks on the northern end of Mount Massive. At around 2.2 miles, we'll continue past the junction with the middle leg that connects both the Tree Line and Powderhound loops and trek just a bit farther to where the trail arrives at the far end of the parking lot and the trailhead.

56 | JACKAL HUT

Round trip ■	9.1 miles
Loop direction ■	Counterclockwise
Hiking time ■	6.5 hours
Sweat factor ■	High
Starting elevation ■	9295 feet
High point ■	11,710 feet
Low point ■	9275 feet
Elevation gain ■	2415 feet
Best hiking season ■	December through March
Maps ■	USGS Vail Pass; USGS Redcliff
Contact ■	White River National Forest; 10th Mountain Division Hut Association

Driving directions: To reach the trailhead from Leadville, follow US 24 north to South Camp Hale. Look for the first parking area along the highway and start here. The trail crosses the Eagle River and follows East Fork Road.

High in the mountains between Vail and Copper Mountain is the Vail Pass Recreation Area, 50,000 acres of some of the most beautiful land in the state. This trail takes us through the Camp Hale Basin, home in 1942 to some 11,000 soldiers who were training to fight effectively in the European mountain ranges during World War II. From the open basin, the route climbs into mixed forest, through open meadows, and up to the Jackal Hut, with some of the best views this side of the Mississippi. The Collegiate Peaks, Mount Elbert, Mount Massive, Mount of the Holy Cross, the Gore Range, and the Tenmile-Mosquito Ranges all vie for attention on this hike. The Vail Pass Recreation Area requires a $6 per-person fee, 95 percent of which goes right back into the land for maintenance and preservation, and use of the Jackal Hut requires reservations with the 10th Mountain Division Hut Association. Maps and avalanche updates can be found at the parking area, but be sure to double check with rangers concerning avalanche activity.

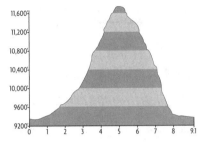

The Vail Pass Recreation Area is a multiuse area offering a chance to avoid the high prices and crowds at the nearby ski areas. Snowmobiling, dogsledding, cross-country skiing, and snowshoeing are all ways to take advantage of the area, and the huts are an added bonus. From the parking area, we'll strike out east across this open basin. Beyond the immediate mountains directly ahead, we can already see bits and pieces of the Mosquito Range in the distance. This wide trail leads to a short wooden bridge over the Eagle River. The river crossing is marked by blue diamonds posted throughout the loop so we don't get hopelessly lost. At 0.45 mile, turn right onto the wide, multiuse trail (East Fork Road) leading to the far eastern edge of this huge basin. On sunny weekend days during the winter, this area gets crowded; snowmobiles are all over the place, and you might even see an occasional dogsled cruising around. We continue east on this trail to the north side of the valley and the dazzling peaks of the Gore Range.

At 0.75 mile is the junction with Ranch Creek Road 9, the return trail for the loop. Keep heading straight on East Fork Road. The valley narrows with dense stands of lodgepole and fir mixed with patchy groves of aspen.

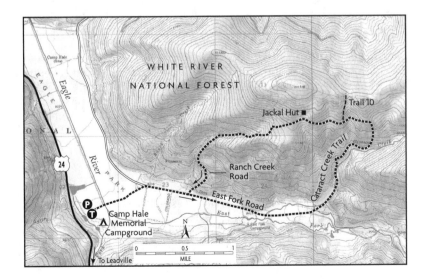

Jackal Hut

A glance behind reveals a couple of peaks just visible in the distant west: Notch Mountain and Mount of the Holy Cross, old friends from hikes earlier in the book. There is a fork in the trail at 1.9 miles, and we will continue moving east as the valley tapers even further, and at 2.7 miles is the junction with the Cataract Creek Trail. Look for the blue diamond indicating Trail 11 and the logo for the Colorado Trail, and turn left off of the multiuse trail onto the CT. The path descends to the bottom of this south-facing hill, turns back to the east, and starts to climb sharply up a steep hill into a huge stand of aspen. Behind us, the valley floor stretches out toward US 24 and even better views of Mount of the Holy Cross. The Tenmile Range is in fine form to the east, and from this bluff we will climb north into a dense grove of aspen—ghost trees standing silent in deep winter white. The trail gets steeper as we push north and follow a shallow gorge into a valley, cross over a little creek, and start climbing again. It is a peaceful scene, and blissfully quiet, with soft mounds of snow in the trees and minarets of rock rising high to the north. Animal tracks scatter everywhere as the trail arcs through this open area, ascending steeply along several switchbacks into another enormous valley buttressed by a steep slope on the left. Now our route follows the contours of the mountain, allowing for a gentler ascent, and we are treated to great views of the Tenmile Range, the peaks of Holy Cross Wilderness, and the Mount Massive area to the southwest. Keep your eyes peeled for the blue diamonds and arrows marking the way. (The authors won't admit it, but there is a chance they got good and lost right about here.)

At 4.2 miles, we have reached the far end of the loop and the trail curves back to the west in the direction of the hut, cresting a small knoll before descending to a saddle and the junction with Trail 10. We'll sail right past the junction and make the final climb up to the Jackal Hut. The hut rests on a bald spot of this mountain at 11,680 feet. The beautiful log cabin has room for sixteen guests and there is easy access to excellent snowshoeing and cross-country and telemark skiing right outside the door. Our trail continues above the hut and cuts right over the top of the mountain at about 5.5 miles. From this vantage, we get some of the paramount views in the state. To the north are rugged peaks of the Gore Range; to the east, the Tenmile Range extends south; in the west is Mount of the Holy Cross; and south of it are the big boys, stalwart Mount Massive and Mount Elbert, the highest point in the state at 14,433 feet. And even farther south are the distant summits of the Collegiate Peaks. Wow—so much alpine splendor on one trail. It doesn't get much better than this.

Next time, we should plan on staying at the Jackal Hut, but for now we begin a long descent to the west, immersed in a big forest resplendent with lodgepole pine. The trail is somewhat steep as it winds down through the trees. This is play time for hardy souls who schlepped skis up the other side—glade skiing at its finest. The descent is long and can be arduous to aching legs, but eventually glimpses of the Camp Hale Basin come back into view. The trail negotiates a few more long switchbacks through another pretty stand of aspen, and at 8.3 miles, Trail 9 reaches its end at the wide trail we started on. Hang a right onto East Fork Road and amble back to the trailhead to close this spectacular hike.

57 HIGHLINE LOOP

Round trip	■	7.1 miles
Loop direction	■	Counterclockwise
Hiking time	■	4.5 hours
Sweat factor	■	High
Starting elevation	■	9650 feet
High point	■	10,989 feet
Low point	■	9645 feet
Elevation gain	■	1350 feet
Best hiking season	■	December through April
Maps	■	USGS Leadville North
Contact	■	San Isabel National Forest

Driving directions: To reach the trailhead, drive west out of Leadville on US 24 for 3 miles. Turn right onto Colorado 300 for 2 miles to the

Leadville National Fish Hatchery on the left side of the road. The trail begins at the visitor center.

Nestled at the base of Mount Massive, Colorado's second highest mountain, the Highline Loop is a glorious snowshoe hike deep in the quiet woods southwest of Leadville. The hike forms a triangle combining the Rock Creek Trail, the Colorado Trail, and the Highline Trail to create the loop. We are enveloped in dense stands of lodgepole pine the entire way, every now and again stealing peeks toward the gnarly heights of Mount Massive and Mount Elbert. The trail begins with a long stretch of gently rolling forest, finishes with a fun, cruising descent, and is only interrupted by one challenging stretch of climbing that will test your strength and warm your bones no matter how cold it may be out there.

After signing in at the trail register, let's trek southeast on wide Road 108 through abundant lodgepole pine, gradually gaining elevation to the first of a cluster of lakes used by the fish hatchery. Established in 1889, this federal hatchery is the second oldest in existence! The hatchery continues to replenish the once-threatened native greenback cutthroat trout and stocks fish for anglers throughout the Rocky Mountain region. At this first lake, take a right toward the sign indicating a picnic area. From this point on, we'll follow the trail marked by blue diamonds. The trail wraps to the west

side of the lake, with jaw-dropping views of Mounts Massive and Elbert, to a second junction at another lake marked by a historical sign. The sign

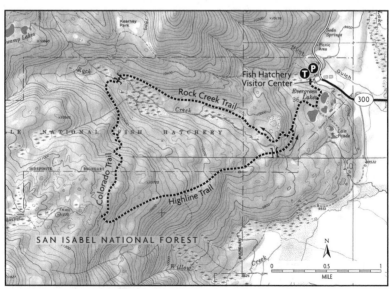

declares that this is the former site of the Evergreen Lake Hotel, a stately hideaway for the well-to-do in the 1880s that burned to the ground. From the junction, we will continue west along the shore of the lake and at 0.4 mile take a right turn toward a sign leading to the trifecta of trails: the Highline Trail, the Rock Creek Trail, and the Colorado Trail. The path makes a large arc northwest deep into the forest and then turns back south. At 0.8 mile, we make a right turn at the sign announcing the Colorado Trail, and start the loop by heading west.

Thus begins the first leg of this triangular hike, climbing west through the trees and a landscape littered with boulders on the Rock Creek Trail, in the direction of the epic Colorado Trail. After one large switchback, the trail passes another junction at 1.2 miles, and we will keep heading straight to the west on a parallel course with Rock Creek. From here, the trail continues over a broad, flat plain blanketed by trees that sporadically reveal previews of the huge mountains so close to us. The presence of these colossal

Bridge of snow on the Highline Loop

mountains is powerful and exciting—we can *feel* them out there beyond the trees. At 1.4 miles, we pass by the sign for Mount Massive Wilderness and continue moving west along the large gorge funneling Rock Creek. This section of the hike is gentle, marked by terraces and plateaus of land with easy transitions in between. Don't get used to it though; this section is merely a warm-up for the big push.

At 2.55 miles, the Rock Creek Trail ends at the junction with the Colorado Trail. This will be a left turn and the start of the second and most difficult leg of the loop. We'll work our way down to the creek and cross over the small wooden bridge. This is a great spot to open a thermos of hot chocolate and listen to the creek gurgling beneath the ice before we begin the big climb. This is a little-used section of the Colorado Trail, and it is important to keep a sharp eye out for the blue diamonds marking the path; some stretches are easy to follow, others may require some attentive orienteering. From here, the trail hooks west and starts to rise steeply to the south on a straight course, gaining elevation in a big hurry. It seems the higher we go, the more prevalent that delicious feeling of true isolation becomes. Here we are on the flanks of Mount Massive, the second highest peak in Colorado, snowshoeing through the depths of an enchanting forest, in perfect alpine silence. At 3.1 miles, the steep, straight path gives way to three or four switchbacks that take us ever higher. After the switchbacks, the path straightens again and climbs onto a large knoll concealing Native Lake near the 4-mile point, marking the high point of this trek. Yikes, that mile and a half included around 1500 feet of our elevation gain for the whole trip! Time to relax by the lake and rehydrate.

We part ways with the Colorado Trail at a junction on the southwest side of the lake, turning left on the Highline Trail and heading east on the last leg of the triangle. (At the time of this writing, there was no sign indicating the Highline Trail. Use your compass and make sure you follow the trail leading east.) The trail descends sharply off the knoll and eases into a more gradual grade. Small bends here and there create variations in this otherwise straight course as the path cruises through stands of gaunt pines. This relaxing grade takes us all the way out of the wilderness area at 5.7 miles, then cuts back north to 6.1 miles and crosses over Rock Creek again on another cool wooden bridge. Just past the creek is one last junction; let's turn right and head back to the stem of the loop at 6.4 miles, and follow the path past the hatchery lakes and down to the trailhead to close this great day of 'shoeing.

58 DEADHORSE CREEK

Round trip ■	7 miles
Loop direction ■	Clockwise
Hiking time ■	3.5 hours
Sweat factor ■	Moderate+
Starting elevation ■	9108 feet
High point ■	10,363 feet
Low point ■	9108 feet
Elevation gain ■	2710 feet
Best hiking season ■	December through April
Maps ■	USGS Fraser
Contact ■	Arapaho National Forest

Driving directions: To reach the trailhead from Interstate 70, exit onto US 40 toward Winter Park. Drive through Empire, over Berthoud Pass, through Winter Park, and into the town of Fraser. Turn left at the only stoplight in town, proceed under the railroad bridge, and turn right onto St. Louis Creek Road 160. At the first stop sign, turn left and follow the dirt road until you see signs indicating the Deadhorse Creek trailhead.

This hike takes place in the gorgeous Winter Park–Fraser Valley area. With high-alpine views and densely walled stands of lodgepole pine nestled below the Vasquez and Byers Peak Wilderness Areas, this is a perfect place to strap on snowshoes for some winter fun. Located between Interstate 70 and Rocky Mountain National Park, the Fraser Valley is made to order for outdoor lovers, and this trail is one of its highlights. If you are looking for solitude and an opportunity to break some fresh snow, plan on making the Deadhorse Creek Loop one of your destinations.

Deadhorse Creek Trail heads southwest away from the parking lot, following the sign for the St. Louis Creek and Deadhorse Loop Trails. This is a road during the summer, so the winter trail begins with ample girth as it moves through a large stand of lodgepole pine, Engelmann spruce, and lower-lying willows. Let's stay left at the first unmarked junction and continue up the wide path. The trail mildly ascends among the trees as we pick up the trail of the blue diamond markers that lead the way to 0.4 mile and a signed junction instructing us to turn right toward the Deadhorse Creek Loop. We will descend through moss-draped pines on another wide, multiuse trail; as the adage goes, make sure to expect and respect all other users of the trail networks. Slowly but surely, the trail tilts upward, and approaching mile 1, the trail bends in the first of a few switchbacks and crosses West St. Louis Creek. An adjacent building that appears to be a run-of-the-mill utility shed reminds us that this hike takes place in the Fraser Experimental Forest, established in 1937 for purposes of forest research. The "utility shed" serves as a research station, and similar facilities throughout this 36-square-mile forest are used to study and record information concerning climate, soils, foliage, and wildlife of the area.

Pushing eastward on this long switchback, we are treated to fantabulous views of the west-facing side of the Indian Peaks. Stop for a minute and remember our trip on the Devils Thumb hike (Hike 16); we were high on that ridge right over there on the Continental Divide. Looks pretty humbling from here, eh? Continuing on, the large valley that introduced our trek now drops low off to the right and we appreciate some flatter terrain for a short while, enjoying a look at Bottle Peak jutting up in the west. The level ground is short-lived, however, as a fold in the landscape crosses another drainage and the trail resumes its switchback course to higher elevations. Soon, the Indian Peaks lead our eyes south to the heights of Berthoud Pass. Look carefully

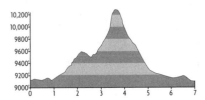

for a tiny box on top of the pass marking an old ski lift. Used primarily as a backcountry ski area now, Berthoud Pass was one of Colorado's first ski resorts. In 1937 an 878-foot rope tow was installed for ambitious skiers looking for adventure.

After one more beautiful bluff, affording the best views all day of the Indian Peaks, we reach 4.6 miles and the far point in the loop. Look for a somewhat indiscernible arrow on the right side of the path, which turns us east onto the Spruce Creek Trail, which immediately submerges into the trees on a much narrower and more intimate path. Spectacular peaks of the Byers Peak Wilderness rise up from the south on this fast and fun descent through the trees. Heading back east now, the trail makes some long, irregular bends to the north and south. Compared to the squirrelly ascent, these switches are longer and steadier. At 5.4 miles, stay right on the Spruce Creek Trail at another unmarked junction. The trail quickly begins to adhere to the contours of the mountainside as it picks up and follows Spruce Creek. The trail bottoms out as Spruce Creek morphs into a large basin off to the right and we walk into a renegade vein of aspen amidst the dense lodgepole woods. Reaching the end of the loop, we return to the sign announcing the

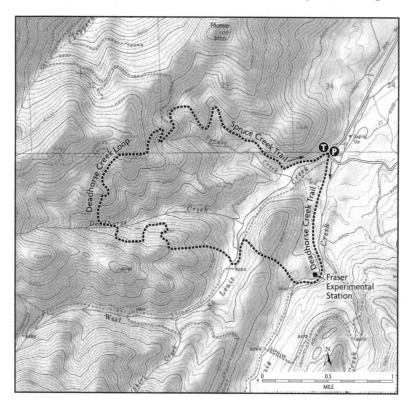

Sunny winter day near Fraser

Deadhorse Loop, immediately followed by a right turn over Spruce Creek and back down the stem trail to the parking area to close this fun hike.

59 10TH MOUNTAIN HUT TRAIL

Round trip ■	**7.3 miles**
Loop direction ■	Clockwise
Hiking time ■	4+ hours
Sweat factor ■	Moderate+
Starting elevation ■	9926 feet
High point ■	11,347 feet
Low point ■	9926 feet
Elevation gain ■	1205 feet
Best hiking season ■	December through April
Maps ■	USGS Leadville North
Contact ■	San Isabel National Forest

Driving directions: To reach the trailhead from Leadville, drive north on US 24 for 7.3 miles and turn left onto the first dirt road past the Sylvan Lakes Estates entrance. Then drive approximately 1 mile until you see the sign for Wurts Ditch and Slide Lake. This marks the beginning of the hike. If the road is impassable due to snow, park at the plowed parking area just off of US 24 and hike the additional mile to the trailhead.

Deep in the mountains of Italy, Riva Ridge posed a formidable line of defense for Mount Belvedere, a major German stronghold during World War II. One night in February 1945, American soldiers scaled the 1500-vertical-foot ridge to surprise a lone German battalion before going on to successfully capture the peak: 1500 vertical feet lugging full combat gear in ice-cold winter darkness—tough hombres, without a doubt. Today's hike takes us to the 10th Mountain Hut, a small cabin near the Continental Divide honoring the heroic men who trained at Camp Hale as part of the U.S. Army's 10th Mountain Division. In 1980, the 10th Mountain Division Hut Association was founded and two backcountry huts were built to provide shelter for cross-country skiers. Today there are twelve huts available for winter and summer use in some of Colorado's most beautiful environs.

Following the path of the blue diamond markers, this lollipop loop begins by heading west on a steady ascent through thick stands of lodgepole. Close to a half-mile in, we'll meet the Continental Divide Trail at a major junction, cross this magnificent alpine path, and follow the sign straight ahead toward the 10th Mountain Division Winter Trail. The trail sneaks through a gate indicating the end of all motor vehicle traffic and winds its way down south through the trees to another path and a sign that says, "Over the snow route." A right turn here leads us along a broad, relatively flat arc to the southwest to the 1-mile mark, where our route joins the Colorado Trail and continues straight toward the Lily Lake Loop. Shortly after, the trail emerges on the southern edge of a large, open basin in the immense West Tennessee Creek drainage. If you listen carefully, you can hear the muffled sounds of a creek tumbling under the snow through the willows that compose this break in the heavy trees. Crossing over a culvert and out of this small valley, the trail begins to rise, gradually moving into an area of trees that have thinned to reveal wonderful views west to the snowcapped tips of the Continental Divide. At the top of a small plateau at just over 2 miles, we find an unmarked junction in a broad basin. Look for a tree on your left with a jumble of one blue and three orange diamonds, and turn right. On a cloudless day during a Colorado winter, the views through this basin are impeccable. The northern reaches of the Holy Cross Wilderness Area create part of the huge bowl of mountains directly ahead. Out east, the craggy fingers of the Tenmile Range point skyward and, more immediately, we are surrounded by the deep greens of conifers and dazzling white of Colorado's trademark

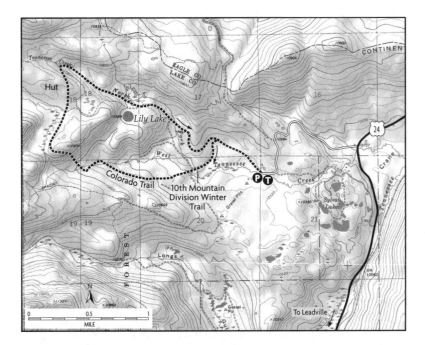

powder. At the far edge of the basin, the trail is again submerged into lodgepole forest, marking the beginning of the long climb of the day, all the way up to the hut. Once in the trees, the trail gets steep enough for a couple of switchbacks and certainly reminds us that snowshoeing is a vigorous workout indeed, especially in fresh snow. But the rewards are truly special, and as the path flirts with tree line, small glimpses of these winter treats materialize through the thick foliage of the pines. Sure enough, as the trail climbs higher, long gaps in the trees reveal some of the best mountain vistas in Colorado. Trailing off south are the resplendent Mounts Massive and Elbert, and in the background the massive Collegiate Peaks rise above Buena Vista. Behind us in the east rest the Tenmile-Mosquito Ranges, creating the eastern edge of the large valley cradling the timeless mountain town of Leadville. And right in front of us rises all 13,209 feet of Homestake Peak and a spectacular bowl of mountains of the Continental Divide.

We have been steadily rising to the west for some time, and the blue diamonds turn us north for the final push to the hut. Approaching 4 miles, the mark of humankind interrupts nature's splendor as the 10th Mountain Division Hut's A-frame peeks through some scattered trees. If we had planned ahead and made the appropriate reservations to stay in the hut, now would be the time to relax, change into some dry, comfortable clothes, and put a big pot of water on the burner for some hot chocolate. But today we will pass by the hut, albeit with more than a little reluctance, and continue due east into high mountain vistas.

The trail generally descends southeast now with smaller twists and turns all over the place, down through this large basin and into the trees again. The blue diamonds guide us through a series of enchanting glades and into open meadows—shade and sunshine, sweeping views and embracing trees. The path gets steep at times and makes for a fun, cruising snowshoe run over small hills and undulations. At 6.3 miles, the trail comes parallel to a gulch and shortly after crosses through a gate and passes a small cabin indicating our next junction. Let's continue straight and follow the gulch to 6.8 miles and the end of the loop portion of the hike. Turn left here onto the stem of the lollipop and retrace this short distance back to the trailhead.

Solitude on the 10th Mountain Hut Trail

60 ┊ SPRAGUE LAKE LOOP

Round trip	■	**2.15 miles**
Loop direction	■	Counterclockwise
Hiking time	■	1.5 hours
Sweat factor	■	Low
Starting elevation	■	8720 feet
High point	■	8839 feet
Low point	■	8688 feet
Elevation gain	■	262 feet
Best hiking season	■	Year-round, but winter recommended
Maps	■	USGS Estes Park; Trails Illustrated, Rocky Mountain National Park
Contact	■	Rocky Mountain National Park

Driving directions: To get here, enter Rocky Mountain National Park on the east side at the Beaver Meadows Entrance. Shortly after the entrance, turn left onto Bear Lake Road, drive for 6 miles, and turn left toward Sprague Lake. Follow the signs to the main parking area; the trail begins at the east side of the parking lot.

From 1910 to 1940, the Sprague Lake area was used as a resort owned by Abner and Alberta Sprague. Just before the inception of Rocky Mountain National Park in 1915, the Spragues dammed the far end of the lake to make it bigger and create better fishing for guests. Today, this lake is a starting point for a number of trails and offers a half-mile, wheelchair-accessible hike around the lake. We chose this popular area as a perfect introduction to snowshoeing, or those snowshoeing with young ones along. The path follows the shores of the lake with breathtaking views of the Continental Divide, into a quiet and soft landscape of snow-covered pines and iced-over creeks, and finishes through a long corridor of lodgepole pine. It is a popular area, but when compared to its busy neighbor, Bear Lake, it will feel like a nice retreat from the crowds.

We will begin our casual venture by cruising southwest from the parking lot over a small wooden bridge toward the lake. Big ponderosas, aspen, and water-dependent willow bushes accent the area as the trail follows a narrow path into the trees. Before long, we come abreast with the lake and move south across a boardwalk accommodated with benches for enjoying views of Sprague Lake and the Continental Divide out to the west. Some of the most beautiful photographs of the park have been shot on the eastern shores of the lake.

Once the trail moves off the

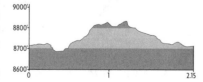

boardwalk and hooks east along the southern edge of the lake, look for orange tags on the trees that mark the path when the snow gets really deep. A lot of snow means a lot of snowshoeing fun. The views of the Divide get better and better toward the far end of the lake. Take a look at the mountains out there—the most distinctive peak, the one that looks like a big cube that has been cut away diagonally from the top, is Hallett Peak at 12,713 feet. Moving to the left are Otis and Taylor Peaks. And moving to the right from Hallett are Flattop and Notchtop Mountains—an impressive display of high ground, to be sure.

Just past some informational plaques around a half-mile in, a trail sign indicates a right turn toward the Glacier Basin Campground. Let's follow this trail off the lake, and typically away from the crowds. The trail moseys down to a creek and wanders east now through the gorgeous pines that have obscured our views of the mountains. The path turns northeast through lodgepole and spruce, and passes by pristine marshmallow mounds of snow that gently slide into the creek and make simple stumps look like extra large mushrooms. Quietly sweeping through this winter wonderland, you would

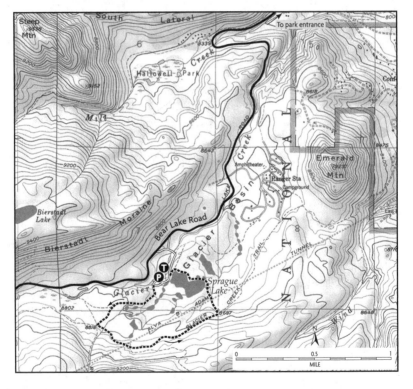

Opposite: View of the Continental Divide on the Sprague Lake Loop

never guess you are so close to one of the most popular roads in the park.

At the 1-mile mark, there is a junction with a number of options. Follow the sign north toward Glacier Basin and Glacier Creek Livery. Soon after, we make a sharp turn left toward Sprague Lake. Views of the mountains open up again as the trail takes us through an open basin and over the creek cutting through the middle of it. Large, wind-ripped mountains to the south act as foothills to Longs Peak, which remains just out of sight. From the basin, the trail plunges back into a canopy of pine trees and begins some gentle undulations creating the negligible elevation gain for this hike. As the trail approaches 1.7 miles, we will pass a large metal shack and emerge onto a road. Let's turn left and move back toward the lake in order to finish up this short hike. Follow the one-way sign and stay right on this road until you see the orange snowshoe markers near the end of the turnaround, which leads back to the lake.

At 2 miles, we arrive back at the lake and are near the end of the loop, which finishes up on the western end of the lake. Take another lap around the lake if your legs still feel good, or explore one of the other nearby trails in this beautiful area of the park.

APPENDIX

City of Boulder Open Space and
Mountain Parks Department
P.O. Box 791
Boulder, CO 80306
(303) 441-3440
www.osmp.org

Boulder County Parks & Open Space
PO Box 471
Boulder, Colorado 80306
(303) 441-3950
www.co.boulder.co.us/openspace

Larimer County Parks and Open
Lands
1800 S. County Road 31
Loveland, CO 80537
(970) 679-4570
www.co.larimer.co.us/parks

Colorado State Parks
Denver Administrative Office
1313 Sherman Street, #618
Denver, CO 80203
(303) 866-3437
www.parks.state.co.us

Colorado State University
College of Natural Resources
Environmental Learning Center
3745 E. Prospect Road
Fort Collins, CO 80525
(970) 491-1661
www.cnr.colostate.edu/elc

USDA Forest Service
Arapaho & Roosevelt National
Forests
2150 Centre Avenue, Building E
Fort Collins, CO 80526
(970) 295-6600
www.fs.fed.us/r2/arnf

USDA Forest Service
White River National Forest
900 Grand Avenue
P.O. Box 948
Glenwood Springs, CO 81602
(970) 945-2521
www.fs.fed.us/r2/whiteriver

USDA Forest Service
Pike & San Isabel National Forests
Cimarron & Comanche National
Grasslands
2840 Kachina Drive
Pueblo, CO 81008
(719) 553-1400
www.fs.fed.us/r2/psicc

USDA Forest Service
Medicine Bow-Routt National
Forests
Thunder Basin National Grassland
2468 Jackson Street
Laramie, WY 82070
(307) 745-2300
www.fs.fed.us/r2/mbr

USDA Forest Service
San Juan National Forest
15 Burnett Court
Durango, CO 81301
(970) 247-4874
www.fs.fed.us/r2/sanjuan

Grand Mesa, Uncompahgre, and
Gunnison National Forests
2250 US Highway 50
Delta, CO 81416
(970) 874-6600
www.fs.fed.us/r2/gmug

National Park Service
Rocky Mountain National Park
1000 Highway 36
Estes Park, CO 80517
(970) 586-1206
www.nps.gov/romo

Garden of the Gods Park
City of Colorado Springs Parks and
    Recreation
1401 Recreation Way
Colorado Springs, CO 80905
(719) 385-5940
www.springsgov.com

Black Canyon of the Gunnison
    National Park
102 Elk Creek
Gunnison, CO 81230
(970) 641-2337
www.nps.gov/blca

Mesa Verde National Park
PO Box 8
Mesa Verde, CO 81330
(970) 529-4465
www.nps.gov/meve

Jefferson County Open Space
700 Jefferson County Pkwy
Suite 100
Golden, Colorado 80401
(303) 271-5925
*www.co.jefferson.co.us/ext/dpt/comm
    _res/openspace*

Florrisant Fossil Beds National
    Monument
P.O. Box 185
15807 Teller County 1
Florissant, CO 80816
(719) 748-3253
www.nps.gov/flfo

Bureau of Land Management
1849 C Street, Room 406-LS
Washington, DC 20240
(202) 452-5125
www.blm.gov

Leave No Trace Center for Outdoor
    Ethics
P.O. Box 997
Boulder, CO 80306
(800) 332-4100
(303) 442-8222
www.LNT.org

INDEX

AUTHOR BIOS

A native of Wisconsin, **Steve Johnson** is a freelance writer and an avid devotee of most any self-propelled activity. A graduate of Colorado State University, he has written about outdoor recreation for publications such as *Bicycling*, *Hooked on the Outdoors*, and *Silent Sports*, and is the author of several outdoor guidebooks. He currently lives with his family in southeastern Minnesota.

David Weinstein was born and raised in Boulder, Colorado. He has worked on trail crews for the city of Boulder, volunteered for the Continental Divide Trail Alliance, and remains an active outdoor enthusiast. He graduated from Colorado State University and is currently teaching English in Japan.

Steve Johnson

David Weinstein

THE MOUNTAINEERS, founded in 1906, is a nonprofit outdoor activity and conservation club, whose mission is "to explore, study, preserve, and enjoy the natural beauty of the outdoors. . . . " Based in Seattle, Washington, the club is now the third-largest such organization in the United States, with seven branches throughout Washington State.

The Mountaineers sponsors both classes and year-round outdoor activities in the Pacific Northwest, which include hiking, mountain climbing, ski-touring, snowshoeing, bicycling, camping, kayaking, nature study, sailing, and adventure travel. The club's conservation division supports environmental causes through educational activities, sponsoring legislation, and presenting informational programs.

All club activities are led by skilled, experienced instructors, who are dedicated to promoting safe and responsible enjoyment and preservation of the outdoors.

If you would like to participate in these organized outdoor activities or the club's programs, consider a membership in The Mountaineers. For information and an application, write or call The Mountaineers, Club Headquarters, 300 Third Avenue West, Seattle, WA 98119; 206-284-6310. You can also visit the club's website at *www.mountaineers.org* or contact The Mountaineers via email at *clubmail@mountaineers.org*.

The Mountaineers Books, an active, nonprofit publishing program of the club, produces guidebooks, instructional texts, historical works, natural history guides, and works on environmental conservation. All books produced by The Mountaineers Books fulfill the club's mission.

Send or call for our catalog of more than 500 outdoor titles:

The Mountaineers Books
1001 SW Klickitat Way, Suite 201
Seattle, WA 98134
800-553-4453
mbooks@mountaineersbooks.org
www.mountaineersbooks.org

OTHER TITLES YOU MIGHT ENJOY FROM
THE MOUNTAINEERS BOOKS

100 Classic Hikes in Colorado
Scott Warren
Gorgeous color, fully detailed, best-selling hiking guide to Colorado.

Best Hikes with Dogs: Colorado
Ania Savage
80 hikes selected to delight your dog (and you) throughout Colorado—many accessible from urban areas.

Best Hikes with Children: Colorado
Maureen Keilty
Short hikes for young hikers (and those still young at heart) in Colorado.

Hiking Colorado's Geology
Ralph Hopkins and *Lindy Hopkins*
Hikes that lead you to an understanding of the unique and spectacular geologic formations of Colorado.

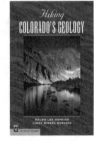

Snowshoe Routes:
Colorado's Front Range
Alan Apt
A complete snowshoeing guide to Colorado's most popular winter sports region.

Available at fine bookstores and outdoor stores, by phone at 800-553-4453 or on the web at *www.mountajneersbooks.org*

THE MOUNTAINEERS BOOKS